Best · Hikes
CHILDREN®
in Western &
Central Oregon

Best Hikes With CHILDREN®
in Western & Central Oregon

by Bonnie Henderson

THE
MOUNTAINEERS

For Molly Wilson, in memory of her dad, Peter

0 9 8 7 6
7 6 5 4 3

Published by The Mountaineers
1001 SW Klickitat Way, Seattle, Washington 98134

Published simultaneously in Canada by Douglas & McIntyre, Ltd., 1615 Venables Street, Vancouver, B.C. V5L 2H1

Published simultaneously in Great Britain by Cordee, 3a DeMontfort Street, Leicester, England, LE1 7HD

Manufactured in the United States of America

Edited by Linda Gunnarson
Maps by Carla Majernik
Cover design by Betty Watson
Book layout by Constance Bollen
Cover photograph by Paul D. Hoobyar
All photographs by Bonnie Henderson, except the following: Michael S. Thompson, pages 27, 149, 151, 187, 201, 226, 232, 245, 252; Richard Goss, page 166; David Falconer, page 34; Paul D. Hoobyar, pages 2, 124, 152, 155, 169, 181, 202, 247
Frontispiece: Above Punch Bowl Falls on Eagle Creek

Library of Congress Cataloging-in-Publication Data
Henderson, Bonnie
    Best hikes with children in Western and Central Oregon / by Bonnie Henderson.
      p.   cm.
    Includes index.
    ISBN 0-89886-319-8
    1. Hiking—Oregon—Guide-books.   2. Family recreation—Oregon—Guide-books.   3. Oregon—Description and travel—1981-—Guide-books.   I. Title.
GV199.42.07H46   1992
917.95—dc20   91-41330
                                            CIP

Contents

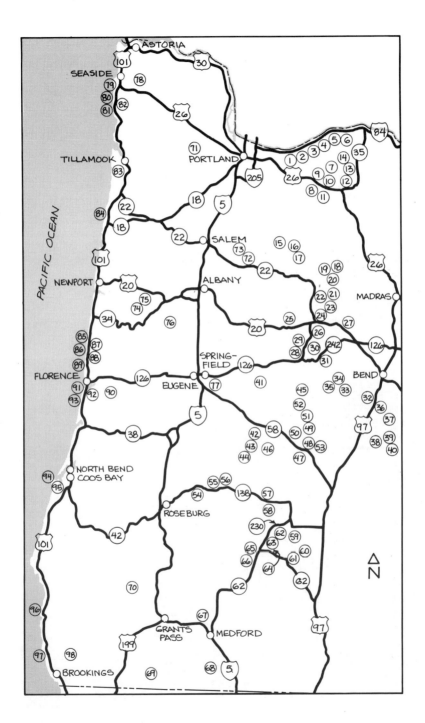

Acknowledgments

Thanks to all the national forest and state parks personnel who offered advice on trails, based on both their professional knowledge and their personal experience with their own children.

Thanks, Mom, and all the friends who watched John, or who accompanied me on hikes, or both.

Thanks, John, for putting up with more time in the backpack than you probably would have chosen.

Thanks to my doctors, for giving me back the gift of walking.

Thanks to my parents, who nurtured a love of woods and words.

Thanks, Paul, for all your support.

A NOTE ABOUT SAFETY

Safety is an important concern in all outdoor activities. No guidebook can alert you to every hazard or anticipate the limitations of every reader. Therefore, the descriptions of roads, trails, routes, and natural features in this book are not representations that a particular place or excursion will be safe for your party. When you follow any of the routes described in this book, you assume responsibility for your own safety. Under normal conditions, such excursions require the usual attention to traffic, road and trail conditions, weather, terrain, the capabilities of your party, and other factors. Keeping informed on current conditions and exercising common sense are the keys to a safe, enjoyable outing.

The Mountaineers

KEY TO SYMBOLS

 Easy trails. These are relatively short, level, gentle trails suitable for small children or first-time hikers. Hiking boots are often unnecessary, except to keep feet dry.

 Moderate trails. Most of these are 3 to 5 miles round-trip distance and have an elevation gain of more than 500 feet. The trail may be rough and uneven in places. Hikers should wear lug-soled boots.

 Difficult trails. These trails are generally at least 5 miles round-trip distance and involve considerable elevation gain. The route may be rough and uneven. These trails are suitable for older or experienced children. Lug-soled boots are a necessity.

 Hikable. The best times of year to hike each trail are indicated by the following symbols: flower—spring; sun—summer; leaf—fall; snowflake—winter.

 Driving directions. These paragraphs tell you how to get to the trailheads.

 Turnarounds. These are places where families can cut a hike short yet still have a satisfying outing. Turnarounds usually offer picnic opportunities, views, or special natural attractions.

 Cautions. These mark potential hazards—cliffs, stream crossings, and the like—where close supervision of children is strongly recommended.

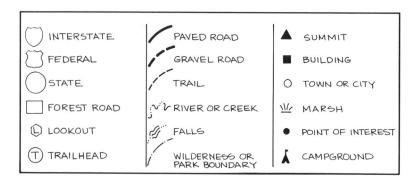

INTERSTATE	PAVED ROAD	▲ SUMMIT
FEDERAL	GRAVEL ROAD	■ BUILDING
STATE	TRAIL	O TOWN OR CITY
FOREST ROAD	RIVER OR CREEK	MARSH
LOOKOUT	FALLS	● POINT OF INTEREST
TRAILHEAD	WILDERNESS OR PARK BOUNDARY	CAMPGROUND

Introduction

Can you remember your very first hike? I can't—I was too young. But I know the story: it was an overnight into Bagby Hot Springs, then 6 miles from the trailhead. I wore ankle-high leather boots with cleated cord soles and carried a little red cotton knapsack handed down from my sister. I was six years old. I know that, because the details of that hike, and of the first hikes of each of my siblings, have become part of family lore, preserved alongside those of other childhood milestones.

I was lucky that my growing-up years were filled with trips into the wilderness. But looking back now, I tend to place these adventures in two categories: goal-oriented hikes and exploratory hikes. The first category included a slog up a steep scree slope on a blazing summer day and portions of a backpack trip in Idaho that I remember as too long and, again, too hot. The second category was pure magic: wandering awestruck in a cathedral-like old-growth forest, fording creeks on fallen logs and pursuing orange-bellied salamanders across the mossy forest floor, backpacking into a hidden lake so full of trout we could pick the fish we'd have for dinner even before we cast.

This book's purpose is to help you create family outings that fall into that second category. The following approaches have helped other adults create memorable outings for their kids; I suggest you try them on yours.

Remember that not all three-year-olds fit size-3 pajamas. Children's readiness for hiking is just as variable. Your kids will let you know when they're ready for a new challenge.

No siblings? "Adopt" some! The extra hassle of taking more children on a hike is generally outweighed by the greater level of cooperation and plain fun your own child is likely to have with a friend or two along.

Assign an "engine" and a "caboose" and rotate these roles. The child in front, setting the pace, enjoys the perks—and a taste of the responsibility—that come with leadership. The "caboose" has the important job of ensuring that no one falls far behind (and, in the process, can feel as important as the "engine").

Take plenty of snacks—even for a half-hour outing. Children need the energy boost, and snacks—carefully rationed—can help keep enthusiasm high.

Be generous with praise. It can do more to raise energy levels than all the granola bars in the world.

Balance new hikes with old favorites. Children often love returning to favorite spots; vary the experience by going in different seasons or at different times of day. Choose trails with special attractions scattered at intervals; as your children grow, so may the distances they hike.

Be a tortoise, not always a hare. Slowly, with lots of stops to catch grasshoppers or poke under rocks, your tortoises will usually get there. They may balk if required to travel at your adult hare's pace.

Encourage a family wilderness ethic. By pointing out indiscretions of other hikers—an empty pop can beside the trail, shortcuts worn between switchbacks—and explaining why your family doesn't do that, you enlist your children as conservationists before it occurs to them to cut across that switchback themselves.

Recognize that exercise is an acquired taste. Reaching target heart rate has little allure for children. When you're out with the kids, be willing to take it slow; get your workout at some other time.

Remember your real goal. Is it to reach the summit of a particular mountain, or to nurture your children's curiosity and sense of adventure and instill a love of the outdoors that will last a lifetime? The patience you demonstrate while the kids tarry over a mysterious hole in the ground, or while they stop—again—to rest and snack, will reward you many times over.

"LET'S GO AGAIN!"

Those words are music to the ears of adults eager to get children interested in the outdoors. And it's really not hard to have a good time; children are naturally energetic, curious, playful—qualities adults often find reemerging in themselves on outings in the wilds. Yet so many little things can potentially spoil a hike, especially for youngsters new to the outdoors whose tolerance for cold, heat, fatigue, bugs, and even long car rides can be limited at best.

A parent's first job is to choose trails carefully. The trails in this book were selected for their interest as well as their relative ease—children may go farther on a difficult, but interesting, trail than on a flat, but boring, trail. Most of the trails lie close to main roads and don't require a tedious drive on gravel logging roads. They were also chosen with an eye toward geographical balance. Hence, many excellent trails were omitted. This book truly offers a selection of the best trails in western and central Oregon; it is not intended to be a complete listing of the best.

All the trails included in this guide go no farther than 1.5 miles without a treat of some kind: a waterfall, a bridge, a lake, a great view, and in one case a crawl-through tunnel. That way, if hikers go no farther than this turnaround point, everyone is still guaranteed a good time and can feel they've accomplished something. This guide steers away from view hikes that require a long uphill slog before offering any reward. By the time a child is ready to switchback 4 miles up a relatively uninteresting trail to reach a stellar viewpoint, you no longer need this book.

HOW TO USE THIS BOOK

This guide covers hikes in western Oregon, an area extending from the Columbia Gorge in the north to the Siskiyous in the south, and from the Pacific Coast eastward to the crest of the Cascades, plus several hikes on the eastern slope of the Cascades. The hikes are grouped geographically in sections keyed to river drainages or mountain passes. Some hikes stand by themselves, but in most cases several hikes are clustered around a major highway, giving car campers several choices for day trips during a family vacation.

For a toddler, the best beginning hike may be a walk in a park a few miles from home, and Portland in particular has a wealth of woodsy parks crisscrossed by gentle trails, particularly Forest Park and Tryon Creek State Park. In Eugene, the Ridgeline Trail and the hike up Spencer Butte are good (and popular) choices for family hikes virtually in town. However, this book includes only trails well beyond city limits. Some are located in the Cascades, but others are low-elevation trails accessible year-round, including many on the coast and in the Willamette Valley.

Selecting a Hike

Read through each trail description in an area that interests you before selecting a hike. A trail rated difficult, for example, may be easy and full of interest for the first mile, making that section a good choice for beginning hikers; one listed as heavily used may actually receive light use except during wildflower season.

Type: All the hikes in this book are short enough to be enjoyed as "dayhikes," meaning one-day or partial-day outings. If a hike is listed as a dayhike, that means overnighting is impractical (due to rough terrain, lack of water, etc.), inadvisable (due to a delicate environment or overuse), or prohibited. "Dayhike or backpack" means the trail is a good choice for an overnight backpacking trip with young children.

Difficulty: The designation of a trail as easy, moderate, or difficult takes into consideration the trail condition, elevation gain, and distance to the major destination. Often children can travel a long distance on level trails, especially if there are interesting distractions along the way. Given the opportunity to pause and explore, kids tend to find interesting stuff everywhere. Add some elevation gain and long stretches without much variation in scenery, and the fatigue level goes up quickly. More than half the hikes in this book are judged easy. If a short hike is what you're after, don't limit your choices to the easy hikes; most of the moderate and difficult trails have turnaround points. Remember that your own judgment must be added to the formula as well; a ridgeline trail that's a breeze on a balmy June day can quickly turn into a nightmare in blistering heat or persistent rain, especially with very young, tired, or inexperienced children.

Distance: For each hike, the total mileage for the outing is listed. A "round-trip" hike's mileage is the total distance to the destination and back out. A "loop" hike's mileage includes the loop distance and any walking necessary to reach the start of the loop. "One-way" hikes are those with trailheads accessible by car at either end. With a shuttle car, you can make these one-way hikes in one direction only (most appealing when the hike is downhill); if you intend to walk from one end to the other without the shuttle car, hike mileage will double.

Hikable: This line indicates the months the trail is snow-free in a typical year, though the actual hiking season will vary from year to year according to snowpack and weather conditions.

Use: Designations here are generally based on records kept by the managing agency (such as the Forest Service). On light-use trails, you may encounter other hikers on a summer Sunday, but you shouldn't encounter crowds. On heavy-use trails, you can expect to run into other hikers even on an off-season weekday morning; on these trails, be especially mindful of the no-trace wilderness ethic, perhaps leaving the dog at home, walking on the trail and not on fragile trailside meadows, and otherwise taking care to leave as little evidence of your passing as possible.

High point: This number indicates the height above sea level of the highest point on the trail section described.

Elevation gain: This number reflects the total number of vertical feet gained during the course of the hike. In the case of one-way hikes heading downhill, the elevation gain number actually reflects the elevation lost. In some cases, such as hikes near the beach, the elevation gain number will be larger than the high point number; that's because the trail rises and falls several times, making the cumulative elevation gain actually greater than the trail's high point.

Maps: The name of the appropriate topographical map published by the U.S. Geological Survey (USGS), or the appropriate Green Trails map if available, is listed first, generally followed by a second map reference, such as a National Forest map or trail brochure. For route-finding on foot, topographic maps are the best choice. Contour lines indicate elevation variations, helping you gauge the terrain's steepness (and crucial for finding your way if lost); shadings indicate forests and clearings. These USGS topographic maps are a standard reference, but they're often out of date. Wilderness-area maps from the Forest Service generally include contour lines, making them more useful than the less-detailed National Forest maps, though National Forest maps cover a larger area and are sometimes indispensable for road-finding. The Green Trails and Geo-Graphics maps are especially helpful to Northwest hikers. These independent cartographers' topographic maps are more up to date than USGS topos, though they're currently available only for portions of the northern Oregon Cascades.

Note: Several of the newer trails included in this book do not appear on any standard topo maps; in these cases, the maps in this book may be your best trail guides.

WHAT TO TAKE

"My Own Pack!"

Put a pack on a child and immediately the child knows something special is about to happen. You don't have to put much in it—the less the better, at first—but adults often find they get better behavior and more cooperation from a child wearing a pack; it signals that he or she is a bona fide member of the party, not just a youngster the adults brought along on their outing.

Small packs sized for children are widely available, but a smallish adult's daypack may get used for more years—just don't overload it. Fanny packs are also popular with children. One woman I know adds something special to her grandson's pack every time they take a hike: colorful adhesive bandages, a small flashlight, an emergency whistle.

Boots or Shoes?

Until recently it was tough to find a good, affordable child's hiking boot. Those manufactured by hiking boot companies tended to be overbuilt (and overpriced), and those from children's shoe manufacturers tended to look right but function poorly. Better choices are now available; look for them at sporting goods stores that specialize in hiking.

Sneakers—"athletic shoes," as they're now called—are fine on dry, level trails, especially high-risers with ankle support. But their flat soles offer no help with traction. Buy boots if you plan to do any significant hiking with your child.

All-leather hiking boots for children may be too stiff, especially for the very young. Look for pliable, split-grain leather boots with a soft collar and treat them for water-repellency (or you'll lose one of their primary advantages: keeping feet dry). Combination leather-and-fabric boots tend

Skunk cabbage

to be lighter, though not quite as water-repellent. Stiffer boots may require a breaking-in period; have children wear them around the house first, to make sure they fit, then around the neighborhood before embarking on a major outing. Then, just in case, carry moleskin—and be sure to stop and put it on at the first sign of discomfort.

The Ten Essentials . . .

You say you're planning to hike only 2 miles, and the weather's beautiful? It's still a good idea to make sure the following items are in your daypack, especially when hiking with children. This list, compiled by The Mountaineers, has become an accepted standard for hikers and other outdoor users.

1. Extra clothing. Not necessarily a complete set of clothes, but do take at least one more sweater than you think you'll need and, on all but the sunniest summer days, rain gear. Extra socks are usually a good idea, especially with children. Take lightweight "river shoes" (old sneakers or new watershoes) if children plan to wade at a lake.

2. Extra food. Pack what you plan to eat—and then some, just in case. The traditional hikers' menu consists of high-energy, noncrushable foods that won't spoil too quickly, such as dried fruits, nuts, hard crackers, cheese and dried meats, and—in limited quantities—candy. Fresh fruit is heavier but refreshing. Sandwiches with mayonnaise might spoil or get crushed. Pick foods your children don't ordinarily get, or save certain treats for outings (dried fruit rolls or boxed juices, for example), to make hikes special.

3. Sunglasses. Children of hiking age usually like to wear shades, especially if they've helped pick them out. Encouraging kids to wear sunglasses now (particularly around water and snow) helps reduce their chances of developing cataracts years down the road.

4. Knife. One with various blades and gadgets is particularly useful; keep the main blade sharp.

5. Firestarter. A candle or chemical firestarter of some kind is a lightweight addition to a pack, and it can be a lifesaver if you wind up bivouacking unexpectedly.

6. First-aid kit. Keep it supplied with the basics, plus any special medications your group requires (such as a bee-sting kit, if someone's allergic).

7. Matches. The waterproof kind, available at sporting goods stores, are the safest; in any case, keep them in a secure, waterproof container.

8. Flashlight. Not necessarily the big one you keep in the car; tiny but powerful, waterproof minilights are widely available.

9. Map. Even on short trips. Many of the trails in this book aren't so isolated or complicated to require a map for route-finding, though it's always a good idea to carry one. At the very least, older children may enjoy learning to read maps in the field. Furthermore, maps are often necessary for finding your way on the sometimes complicated network of roads leading to National Forest trailheads.

10. Compass. Useless unless you've learned how to use it with a map.

. . . And Then Some

Mosquito repellent. Nothing can so quickly spoil a hike in the woods than a swarm of pesky, incessant mosquitoes. Early summer—or soon after snowmelt, which varies from place to place—is usually the worst time. Children tend to have even less tolerance for mosquitoes than adults.

The best defense is a mosquito repellent of some kind. Virtually all repellents (except some natural products, which tend to be less effective) use a chemical nicknamed DEET as the active ingredient, but it comes in concentrations ranging from about 30 percent to 95 percent. It's less effective at the low end, but you have to be very careful using it in higher concentrations, especially with kids. I know an adult hiker who was temporarily blinded when dripping sweat drew it into his eyes, and you have to keep it off your hands or it eventually migrates into your mouth (or eyes). I've even seen kids wearing high-concentration "jungle juice" on their legs take the color off vinyl car seats. On the positive side, researchers claim even the high-concentration repellents are safe with proper use, and allergic reactions are fairly rare.

Although prudent use of a strong repellent is the best defense, there are others. Lightweight, long-sleeve shirts and pants help discourage (but don't always stop) the critters. Some hikers carry widths of mosquito netting to use as drapes when they pause for rests.

Water. It's unfortunate, but true: there's really no place in the wilderness where you can drink stream water and be completely safe from *Giardia*. This protozoan, carried by human and animal feces, can cause severe diarrhea of a type that can be hard to diagnose (but easy to treat once it is diagnosed).

For short dayhikes, stick to drinking out of water bottles filled at reliable sources—a home tap or a faucet at the trailhead. On longer outings, the simplest defense is to carry a portable water purifier. Purifiers vary in cost and weight, but there are reasonably priced models available that, used properly, can filter out *Giardia* as well as other impurities and are quite compact and lightweight. Alternatives include boiling water for 20 minutes (using up precious fuel) or treating water with iodine or other chemicals available at hiking stores.

Toilet paper. The first Murphy's Law of Hiking with Children: Regardless of how many potty stops you make beforehand, someone has to "go to the bathroom" within 20 minutes of leaving the trailhead. I like to carry two plastic self-sealing bags, one holding dry toilet paper and the other for used TP. You can bury the used toilet paper, but it's likely to get dug up and scattered by animals. Some people burn their used TP; with children, I suggest simply treating it like other litter. If you don't like the idea of packing out your own soiled toilet paper, think about stumbling across someone else's strewn across the forest floor. Also, be sure to bury feces at least 6 inches deep, far from the trail or water sources. Use a stick to dig or, better yet, carry a lightweight plastic trowel.

Sunscreen. If hiking on an exposed trail, or by water or snow, be sure to carry and use sunscreen. Dermatologists now warn that sunburn on young children can be a precursor to skin cancer years later; conversely, carefully protecting children from sunburn in their early years does a lot to reduce their chances of skin cancer as adults. Some children are allergic to PABA, the active ingredient in most sunscreens; pediatricians suggest using a non-PABA lotion with a sun protection factor (SPF) of 30 or higher. Zinc oxide is a good choice for noses and ears; it's available in colors now, so try face-painting and making a game out of applying it. The colored ointment is just as messy as the old standard white, however.

HITTING THE TRAIL
Setting the Pace

Some people think it's a good idea to pace children, teaching them to conserve energy by not burning out too soon and to learn to go slowly enough to make frequent rest stops unnecessary. It's a valuable skill, especially for older children, who may need help in reaching a goal that might be a bit beyond their reach.

For little ones, however, it's probably better to let them go at their own pace, letting their enthusiasm carry them. In that case, watch carefully for signs of fatigue in order to judge when it's time to turn around. Otherwise it may be a long return hike with someone on your shoulders. Waiting while children investigate every growth of fungus or animal burrow can get tiresome—unless you let their sense of wonder expand your vision of what hiking is all about.

Safety

At one end of the spectrum of hikers' personalities are the grim troopers, whose preoccupation with safety seems to overshadow any fun they might be having along the trail. At the other end are the fun hogs, who wear flimsy shoes and run up mountain trails late in the day with no extra gear and not so much as a spare sweatshirt tied around the waist. Fortunately, there's a wide middle range of hikers, with a love of the outdoors and playful hearts, who cover the basics of safety simply to extend their chances of having an enjoyable hike—and to make sure they survive to do it again.

It's easy to be lulled into complacency by a sunny day, a good trail, and your own physical strength and feeling of competence. But as anyone with any experience knows, the wilderness can be a dangerous place for the unprepared; conditions can change quickly, and accidents do happen. It's not something you want—or need—to dwell on. But you can reduce your chances of disaster by covering two bases. First, be prepared. Learn something about the area you'll be going into and carry adequate emergency supplies. In classes or on the trail with more experienced companions, learn survival skills, including how to use a map and compass. Second, know your limits and those of your party.

All the trails in this guide have been field-checked, but conditions and routes change. The trail ratings (easy, moderate, difficult) are estimations only and should be used as guidelines, not as fact. Good judgment is your most powerful safety tool.

Hypothermia and Heat Exhaustion

When they're excited and having fun, children can go a long time before they realize they've overdone it. In cold, wet weather, as in baking summer heat, it's imperative that adults keep a sharp eye on children to look for signs of these two ailments and attend to preventative measures before symptoms appear.

Hypothermia is a potentially life-threatening drop in core body temperature that most often occurs in cold, wet weather but can occur any time: on a windy spring day, for example, when you stop for lunch and don't bother putting a sweater on your sweat-cooled body. To help prevent hypothermia, wear clothing in layers—wool and polypropylene rather than all cotton—and don't hesitate to peel them off, or pile them back on, as your body temperature fluctuates. Always carry (and wear, when necessary) good rain gear. If someone in your party starts shivering, seems disoriented, has cold, clammy skin, or simply seems listless and whiny, get him moving, get more clothes on him, and get hot liquids into him as quickly as possible. Except on hot summer days, it's a good idea to carry a thermos of hot chocolate or cider—if not in your pack, then waiting back at the car.

Heat exhaustion is as easy to get as it is to prevent. You get it by not taking in as much liquid as you are eliminating, and you prevent it by drinking more water than you may think you need. Most children can't be depended upon to drink as much water as they need on very hot days; it's the adults' responsibility to suggest water stops more often than children think necessary. Give a child her own special water bottle and she's more likely to drink up.

The symptoms of heat exhaustion are deceptively like flu; I've been out with kids who insisted they had the flu but whose symptoms subsided in a matter of minutes once they got treatment for heat exhaustion. Don't expect hot skin; people with heat exhaustion usually have a normal or slightly depressed temperature. If anyone in your party is feeling faint, nauseated, or dizzy and feels his heart beating rapidly, especially if the weather's hot and you suspect he hasn't drunk enough water, get him to lie down in a cool, comfortable place and start sipping, then drinking, fluids—salty fluids if you have them, but anything will help. You should notice rapid improvement.

CREATING A
FAMILY WILDERNESS ETHIC

When I used to take teenagers out hiking in summer, many of them on their first wilderness outing ever, we made a point of indoctrinating them with good trail manners long before we reached the trailhead. Litter, we reminded them, is an absolute no-no; we carried plastic bags to haul out not only our own but others' garbage. Picking or cutting down anything, from wildflowers to mushrooms, was another. Cutting switchbacks was also out; that, we explained, was something done by novices who didn't understand the problems of trail erosion.

Rather than taking an authoritarian stance, we explained that all of these transgressions were committed by people who weren't "real hikers." We weren't worried about our group's trail manners, we explained, because they were "real hikers." By the time we did get on the trail, our kids—all novices—were rolling their eyes and looking exasperated at any sign of poor wilderness etiquette—obviously signs of people who weren't "real hikers."

The same approach may work with your children. If good trail manners are presented ahead of time as part of a family wilderness ethic—"This is the way we do it, because we know about and care about the wilderness"—you're more likely to get cooperation than if you wind up scolding over and over on the trail.

Good manners are especially important to use on the trails in this book. Many are already popular routes, with the attendant problems of overuse. The problems would be minimized if everyone who used the trails made a personal effort to leave as little trace as possible. I suggest leaving the dog at home; he'd probably enjoy being out, but your fellow hikers (and nearby wildlife) may be less than thrilled with him. Also consider not camping overnight at popular destinations; instead, camp outside the area and visit it on day trips. This applies especially to delicate ecosystems of the type found around alpine lakes.

Some of the trails in this book are identified as light-use routes; they may be new, or off the beaten path, or simply not well known. I encourage you to try them out; one may wind up a family favorite, and you'll have the satisfaction of knowing that you're helping to disperse the impact of human presence in the natural areas of the Northwest.

HIKING WITH BABIES

As some photos illustrate, I scouted many of these hikes with my son, from age six months to two years, on my back. Modern baby carriers have opened up a whole world of potential family hiking fun—and potential disasters. They enable parents who are avid hikers to continue their

Sheep gridlock near Black Butte

outings even with young children in their lives. Sometimes, however, babies are dragged out onto the trail even when it's not in their best interest. A one-year-old gets more out of a couple of hours in the backyard, practicing her new walking skills and investigating grass and bugs, than she does riding in a backpack for two hours.

In John's first year we found hiking with him to be a hassle much of the time. His tolerance for the pack was short, he'd need to nurse or be changed frequently, and we were so concerned about his warmth and comfort when he was tiny that we worried a lot (probably more than necessary), rather than just being able to enjoy ourselves. We were also using a cheap pack with no headrest or support for him and no hip strap for us. We wound up not hiking with him a lot when he was tiny, and I'd suggest that parents of infants not count on lots of family hiking the first year.

In John's second year it was different. For one thing, we spent the money to buy a good pack with hip support for the hiker and a chest strap, comfortable seat, snack pouch, and other amenities for the baby. In addition, John was no longer nursing, and we could hand him little snacks while we walked, which helped his mood. He didn't need to be changed as often, and he tolerated being in the pack for longer periods, often cooing and talking and looking around at the changing landscape. As he became a more competent walker, we'd let him out of the pack at times and make a game of his walking with us.

Still, we found that the best hikes for parents with a baby were short ones—such as many of those listed as easy in this book. My best advice to new parents: buy a good baby pack, choose short trails, and be patient—your baby won't be a baby forever.

SUGGESTIONS?

I've hiked, and in some cases rehiked, all the trails in this book and checked road names and numbers and directions. But changes do occur; trails fall into disrepair, new roads are built or road numbers and names are changed, and old, abandoned trails are rehabilitated. I would appreciate hearing from readers about discrepancies in the hike descriptions and receiving suggestions of other trails that might deserve inclusion in the next edition of *Best Hikes for Children in Western and Central Oregon*. Please write to me in care of The Mountaineers Books, 1001 S.W. Klickitat Way, Suite 201, Seattle, WA 98134.

Columbia Gorge

Interstate 84

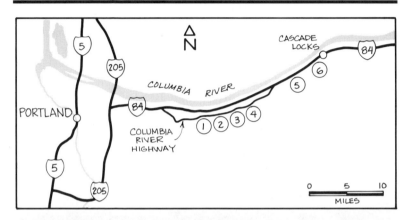

Trailside trillium at Latourell Falls

1. Latourell Falls Loops

Type:	Dayhike
Difficulty:	Easy to moderate
Distance:	1 to 2.2 miles, loop
Hikable:	Most of the year
Use:	Heavy
High point:	700 feet
Elevation gain:	270 to 550 feet
Maps:	Green Trails—Bridal Veil;
	Mount Hood National Forest

As magical as most waterfall-blessed gorge trails are, this one seems even more like a path through a fairyland, with butterflies dancing above pink bleeding hearts and white trilliums blooming on the lush, green hillsides. Little footbridges and a huge natural amphitheater make the gorge at the falls' base particularly impressive. The trail is formed like a figure eight; for a supershort hike, follow just the lower loop. Hike the lower loop clockwise to save the best for last.

From Portland, take I-84 east to exit 28 (Bridal Veil) and backtrack west on the old Columbia River Highway 3 miles to the parking area and overlook at the base of 249-foot Latourell Falls. Left of the falls, an asphalt

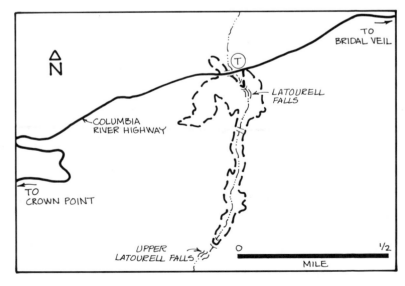

Latourell Falls

path leads up the hill a short distance to a viewpoint. From here, the trail quickly turns to dirt, leading to a second overlook near the top of the falls.

Drop down (passing under a quirky tree overhanging the trail) to a footbridge not far above the falls. Suggest that kids stand on the bridge and close their eyes, not only to hear but to feel the rumbling falls in their feet. If your party is game, backtrack a few steps to a trail junction, turn right, and follow the trail up along the east side of the creek about 0.5 mile to the footbridge at the base of Upper Latourell Falls. The trail continues down the west side of the creek to meet the lower trail just west of the lower falls footbridge.

From here, the trail drops down to the highway at a picnic area 0.2 mile west of the parking area. Rather than return on the road, cross it, drop down some steps and a couple of switchbacks, then bear right, following an asphalt path under the highway and over a footbridge at the base of the falls. Linger a while in this magnificent basalt amphitheater before continuing up to the parking area.

2. Angels Rest

Type:	Dayhike
Difficulty:	Moderate to difficult
Distance:	4.5 miles round-trip
Hikable:	Most of the year
Use:	Heavy
High point:	1600 feet
Elevation gain:	1400 feet
Maps:	Green Trails—Bridal Veil; Mount Hood National Forest

Most trails in the steep-walled Columbia Gorge are steep; those selected for this book require less climbing than most and offer more interesting trailside attractions. Angels Rest is an exception, requiring a pretty strenu-

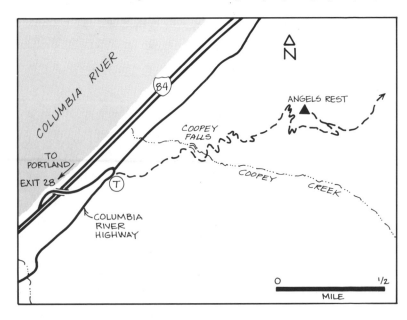

ous climb without many attractions along the way. Rewards include an opportunity to spy rock-dwelling pikas and a view even hard-to-impress children will remember. The hike is best for older children who, once on top, can be trusted to stay away from the precipitous cliff.

From Portland, take I-84 east to exit 28 (Bridal Veil). Take the exit road uphill 0.25 mile to its junction with the old Columbia River Highway and then park. The trailhead (unsigned) is just across the road.

Climb steadily up a forested slope, crossing the creek above Coopey Falls and peeking through the trees at a view of the gorge that grows grander as you ascend. At about 0.4 mile you'll pass through a scree slope, home to a colony of pikas, furry critters about 6 inches tall that are related to rabbits; you may hear their shrill call if you're quiet and search the rocks carefully (with your eyes).

Near the top, switchback several times before reaching a plateau at 2 miles. Turn left and follow a spur trail 0.25 mile out onto the rocky outcrop called Angels Rest. The view is wonderful from either side of the

Angels Rest Trail, with Columbia River beyond

rock, but it's more level—safer—on the east side.

Driving back to Portland, either return via the Bridal Veil interchange or continue up the old Columbia River Highway to Crown Point, a historic landmark building and viewpoint on the rim of the gorge. Continue to Corbett, where the road drops down and leads back to I-84.

3. Multnomah Falls–Wahkeena Falls Loop

Type:	Dayhike
Difficulty:	Moderate
Distance:	3.25 miles, loop
Hikable:	Most of the year
Use:	Heavy
High point:	900 feet
Elevation gain:	1000 feet
Maps:	Green Trails—Bridal Veil;
	Mount Hood National Forest

Most visitors to Oregon's most popular tourist attraction don't wander any closer to 611-foot Multnomah Falls than the top of the stone steps above the Multnomah Falls Lodge. Some take the asphalt path a short distance farther, to the bridge spanning the creek below the falls. Fewer

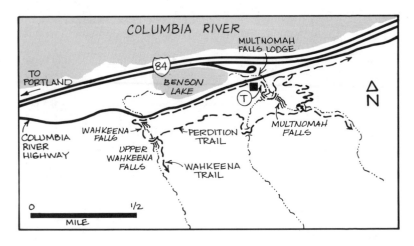

View from the top of Multnomah Falls

still follow that asphalt path all the way to the overlook at the top of the falls—a 1-mile uphill trek. For children, the hike to the top of the falls provides a sense of accomplishment and even identification with a natural landmark that most people know only through postcards.

It's an achievable adventure, one made even more memorable by returning via a wonderfully varied loop route following a forest path along the ridge west of the falls, dropping down past more waterfalls, and returning to the lodge. This is one of several loop trips possible from the falls. To get most of the elevation gain out of the way in the beginning, walk clockwise, starting with the hike to the top of the falls.

From Portland, take I-84 east to exit 31 (Multnomah Falls), park, and walk under the freeway to the lodge. (Or take the old Columbia River Highway, which isn't accessible from the freeway at this point; it passes right in front of the lodge.)

Follow the crowd up the path to the right of the falls, cross the bridge, and continue on the asphalt ribbon as it switchbacks up, and up, and up. At 1 mile, a paved spur leads to an overlook platform above the falls' lip, with a view not really of the falls but of the antlike people below. As long as your children aren't prone to unusually daredevilish acts, it's quite safe.

Continuing on the trail (unpaved now), you'll soon cross an old stone bridge. Just across it is a trail junction; bear right onto Perdition Trail. From here, the trail rolls along a ridge for 1.2 miles as if on a dragon's back, with stairs of stone and railroad ties along the way in several places.

Just past the last, longest, steepest set of stairs is the junction with Wahkeena Trail. Bear right, passing Upper Wahkeena Falls.

Asphalt resumes for the 0.5-mile walk to Wahkeena Falls, just above the highway. Cross the creek and follow the tie trail above the highway 0.5 mile (look for a hanging garden of maidenhair fern on your right), emerging at the west end of the Multnomah Falls parking lot.

---

4. Horsetail Falls–Oneonta Falls Loop

Type:	Dayhike
Difficulty:	Easy
Distance:	2.75 miles, loop
Hikable:	Most of the year
Use:	Heavy
High point:	400 feet
Elevation gain:	500 feet
Maps:	Green Trails—Bridal Veil;
	Mount Hood National Forest

Like the Multnomah Falls–Wahkeena Falls Loop, this trail starts at a waterfall and heads up. It's not as high a climb or as long a hike, however, and it offers a lot of interest along the way, including a fun walk *behind* a waterfall.

Upper Horsetail Falls

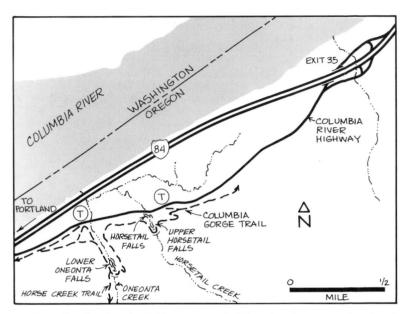

 From Portland, take I-84 east to exit 35 and swing around to head west 1.5 miles on the old Columbia River Highway. (Heading east on the old highway, go 1.5 miles past Multnomah Falls.) Park in the lot across from 176-foot Horsetail Falls, an aptly named narrow cataract.

From the signed trailhead left of Horsetail Falls, head uphill toward Upper Horsetail Falls (also called Ponytail Falls), passing through a garden of maidenhair and other ferns. At 0.25 mile, turn west onto Columbia Gorge Trail and continue another 0.25 mile to the upper falls. (The hill drops away steeply here, but the trail is wide.) Here's where the trail leads behind the falls in a cavelike cleft in the basalt.

 From the upper falls the trail rolls along, offering views of the Columbia and the Washington side of the gorge. At about 0.8 mile the trail starts to drop and soon provides a view down into steep-walled Oneonta Gorge. Switchback down to a bridge crossing Oneonta Creek, listening for the roar of Lower Oneonta Falls below, then head back up briefly to a junction with Horse Creek Trail. Continue west on Columbia Gorge Trail. Proceed another 0.75 mile or so to the last trail junction, head down and east, and follow above the highway, dropping slowly to eventually meet it.

Finish the hike with a 0.5-mile trek back up the old highway. This is probably the most dangerous part of the hike, with narrow road shoulders in places, but cars on the old highway tend to poke along slowly. The accompanying railroad right-of-way, which narrows gradually, is probably more dangerous to walk along than the road shoulder. Be sure to pause at the mouth of Oneonta Gorge for a different perspective on the chasm already seen from above.

5. Wahclella Falls

Type: Dayhike
Difficulty: Easy
Distance: 1.5 miles round-trip
Hikable: Most of the year
Use: Heavy
High point: 380 feet
Elevation gain: 340 feet
Maps: Green Trails—Bonneville Dam;
Mount Hood National Forest

This hike feels so much like a trip into an adventure novel, you may find yourself looking around for the rope swings. Two graceful yet substantial footbridges cross a narrow canyon and rushing creek, with a third bridge hugging the canyon wall at a waterfall-washed cliff face. You'll see wildflowers in spring and maidenhair ferns year-round.

The canyon drops precipitously from the trail in a few places, but the bridges with their triple railings make the hike relatively safe for children. For years this trail was plagued by mudslides and had deteriorated into little more than a scrambler's route. Reconstruction, completed late in 1988, has made it a great family trail, though its adventurous quality remains.

From Portland, take I-84 to exit 40 (Bonneville); turn right, then right

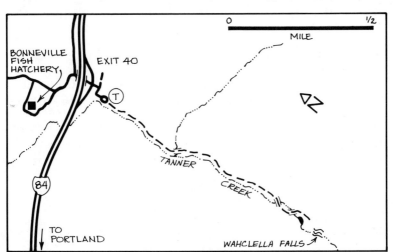

Wahclella Falls

again, following signs a short distance to the cul-de-sac trailhead.

From the trailhead, walk down a service road 0.25 mile to a diversion dam, which directs water to a downstream fish hatchery. At this point the trail narrows to a footpath along the canyon wall. After skirting a small waterfall on the first bridge, notice the basalt columns rising next to the trail. Drop down to a 72-foot bridge crossing Tanner Creek and follow the trail across an old rockslide.

Just before recrossing the creek to reach the falls viewpoint, you'll pass some big boulders standing in shallow pools to your left, an irresistible stopping place for rock-throwers. The falls is a two-tier cataract, dropping perhaps 20 feet to a ledge, then bursting through a rock niche to drop another 60 feet or so into a wide pool. Return the way you came.

Before heading home, consider a visit to the Bonneville Fish Hatchery, just across the freeway from the trailhead. Trout and sturgeon inhabit the display ponds year-round. There are always some fish in the hatchery raceways, too, but most of the action happens the last week in August through the end of November, when hatchery workers can be seen handling spawning Chinook and coho salmon.

6. Punch Bowl Falls

Type:	Dayhike
Difficulty:	Easy to moderate
Distance:	4 miles round-trip
Hikable:	Most of the year
Use:	Heavy
High point:	600 feet
Elevation gain:	240 to 440 feet
Maps:	Green Trails—Bonneville Dam;
	Mount Hood National Forest

There are some hikers who believe children don't belong on Eagle Creek Trail; they say the trail's too slippery and, in places, too narrow, and the canyon too steep. For others, including Forest Service folks with kids of their own, it's at the top of the list of Columbia Gorge hikes for kids. The upshot: don't take a large group of young children here (adults do need to keep an eye on them), nor individual kids who tend to get out of control, and avoid the trail during rainy spells. Otherwise, it's a gem, with a gentle grade, fine views of steep canyon walls, and even a waterfall or two. Understandably, it's also one of the most popular trails in the gorge.

From Portland, take I-84 east to exit 41 (Eagle Creek). Follow the exit road to the fish hatchery, turn right, and follow signs 0.5 mile to the trailhead at the end of the road.

The trail begins as a wide, paved footpath (quickly turning to dirt) following the Eagle Creek's east bank. The trail itself gains elevation faster than the creek, however, gradually taking you higher in the basalt-walled canyon. After about 0.75 mile the trail narrows and grows rockier; a steel cable serves as a hand- and guardrail for about 0.1 mile. Point

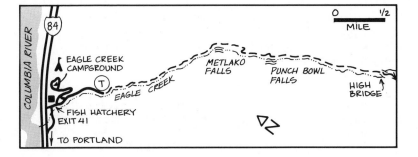

Eagle Creek Trail

out to children (if they don't spot it first) the large cave in the basalt cliff across the canyon.

   After another railed, narrow stretch, the canyon and trail widen, and hikers are surrounded by trees, with the creek out of sight far below but still within earshot.

   A signed spur trail leads to an overlook for Metlako Falls, about 0.25 mile upstream. The spur trail to Punch Bowl Falls is 0.5 mile farther, at 2 miles. It's a steep, rocky, narrow path down to the creek, but the biggest danger is of a child falling on his or her backside and getting muddy. With a drop of only 10 or 15 feet, the falls isn't dramatic, but it is lovely as it pours into a wide pool. The whole scene – a lushly vegetated basalt grotto – is enchanting for adults as well as children and is particularly appealing on a hot day.

   For a longer hike, continue 1.25 miles past the Punch Bowl spur to High Bridge. Here a footbridge crosses the creek, enclosed in a narrow gorge. Eagle Creek Trail continues up Eagle Creek a total of 13 miles to Wahtum Lake.

Mount Hood

U.S. 26 and State 35

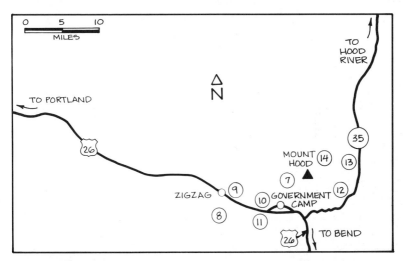

Pine, Douglas fir, and hemlock cones

7. Ramona Falls

Type: Dayhike
Difficulty: Moderate
Distance: 4.4 miles, loop
Hikable: May through November
Use: Heavy
High point: 3300 feet
Elevation gain: 700 feet
Maps: Green Trails—Government
Camp; Mount Hood Wilderness

Popular vote demands Ramona Falls be included in the list of best hikes for children in western Oregon: it's the most well-trammeled trail in Mount Hood Wilderness. Children and adults will like the variety the trail offers, including a memorable footbridge, a tall, lacy falls, and a mossy creek gurgling alongside the trail on the walk out. Consider hiking it in the morning, when the sun isn't yet too hot on Old Maid Flat. Following the loop route described here adds to the hike's interest. (For a less-crowded alternative, see Hike 12, Umbrella Falls–Sahalie Falls Loop.) Dogs are not permitted on this trail.

From U.S. 26, turn north at Zigzag onto Lolo Pass Road (Road 18) and follow it 4.3 miles, turning east onto Road 1825. Continue 2.4 miles and bear left onto Road 100. The spur road to the lower trailhead is on the left in 0.3 mile; the upper trailhead is another 1.6 miles. *Note:* The last mile of road to the upper trailhead is truly horrendous, with car-swallowing potholes and chassis-rattling rocks. At last report it was

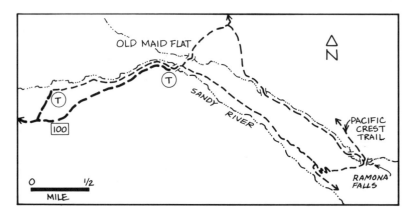

Mount Hood, from Ramona Falls trailhead

passable to passenger cars—barely—but better suited to four-wheel drive. Most people brave the road to save themselves the extra hiking. If you think the kids in your party can handle another 2+ miles of walking, begin hiking in the lower parking area and follow a footpath 1.2 miles to the end of the road. Otherwise, plan on creeping up that last mile. As this book went to press, the Forest Service was considering whether to leave this last mile open or to simply block it off.

At road's end, the trail commences and leads to a tall footbridge—designed to allow room for debris to pass during floods—crossing the Sandy River, milky gray with glacial silt. Immediately you'll reach a junction, the start of the loop route; hike it counterclockwise to get to the falls a little quicker, albeit via a hotter, dustier route. The trail is fairly exposed for the first mile or so, with lodgepole pines lining the route, then enters a cooler grove of Douglas fir. The river itself is rarely in sight but always within hearing distance for the first three-fourths of the hike.

At 1.6 miles the junction with the Pacific Crest Trail (PCT) is reached; turn left and continue 0.5 mile to the falls. Standing in front of Ramona Falls on a hot summer's day is like standing in front of an open refrigerator; the lacy veil of water playing down a face of worn columnar basalt is more like 500 miniwaterfalls, each sending cool air into the falls' amphitheaterlike setting. A split-rail fence at the base (and trampled vegetation all around) suggests that visitors enjoy the falls from a distance—a tall order for kids. Instead, direct them toward playing in the creek below the falls—with supervision.

The loop route continues past the falls (bear left where the PCT heads right) and down a cool vale following moss-banked Ramona Creek, which cries out for children's little bark and leaf "boats" on its drops and pools. About 1.5 miles from the falls, you're in hot lodgepole pine country again for most of the way back. About 1.7 miles beyond the falls, near a trail junction, ask children to be on the lookout for tree wells, formed when lava flowed during an eruption of Mount Hood about 200 years ago and swirled around standing trees. The wood eventually rotted out, leaving molds where the trees had been.

At the junction, bear left. In another 0.6 mile, drop down, cross a creek, and arrive at the start of the loop again. Bear right to recross the Sandy River on the high bridge and get back to the parking area.

---

8. Old Salmon River Trail

Type:	Dayhike or backpack
Difficulty:	Easy
Distance:	2.6 miles one way
Hikable:	March through November
Use:	Heavy
High point:	1640 feet
Elevation gain:	120 feet
Maps:	Green Trails—Government Camp; Mount Hood National Forest

Though it threads a rather narrow corridor between the road and river and isn't exactly remote, the Old Salmon River Trail has a particular charm for families with children. It's wide and virtually level and offers

Old Salmon River Trail

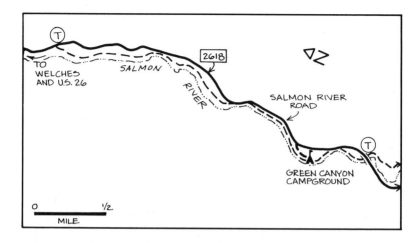

lots of river access. It's also accessible from many points along the road, so you can easily make short, one-way hikes with a second car. And the old-growth forest it traverses has a magical feel, whether the day is sunny or rainy. (The "new" Salmon River Trail begins upstream of this section, where the road crosses and veers away from the river and heads toward Salmon-Huckleberry Wilderness.) There are several campsites along the trail, suitable for a young child's first backpack trip.

Traveling east on U.S. 26, turn right onto Salmon River Road (Road 2618) just west of Zigzag Ranger Station and follow it 2.8 miles to the lower trailhead. The upper trailhead is 2.3 miles farther along this road, just downstream of the concrete bridge crossing the river.

Beginning at the lower trailhead, follow the trail upstream. There are gorgeous, big Douglas firs and huge sword ferns alongside the trail, little footbridges to cross, and lacy cedars sweeping overhead. Bleeding hearts and oxalis carpet the forest floor. The Salmon River itself is particularly appealing on hot summer days, for anglers and others; it's deep green, alternating between deep pools and rocky riffles. Watch wading children carefully, as it is a river with a substantial current.

About a mile from the trailhead, bear right at an apparent fork (and at most other apparent forks; these are generally spurs leading back to the road). At 1.4 miles, the main trail itself leads out to the road at a point where the road is too close to the river to allow room for the trail. Walk along the road for 0.1 mile until the trail resumes and reenters the woods along the river. After walking through a portion of Green Canyon Campground, wind up back along the road once more, briefly, 0.3 mile before the concrete bridge that signals the end of the Old Salmon River Trail.

9. Castle Canyon

Type:	Dayhike
Difficulty:	Moderate
Distance:	1.8 miles round-trip
Hikable:	April through November
Use:	Light
High point:	2200 feet
Elevation gain:	600 feet
Maps:	Green Trails—Government Camp; Mount Hood Wilderness

This hike is recommended only to trail-wise adults and sure-footed children who can follow directions and climb rocks with some care and assurance. It's definitely no place for a baby in a backpack. That said,

Trail's end atop Castle Canyon

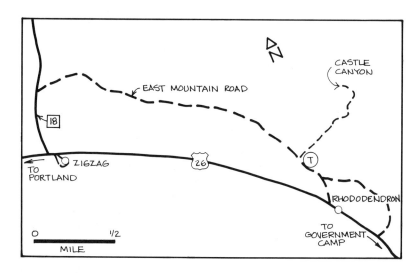

it's a fun, little-known hike to a magical spot atop rock formations of a kind rarely seen on trails around Mount Hood. According to the Forest Service, the larger formations have been given names from Greek mythology—Castle of Hermes and Turret of Polyphemus, for example—but kids will have more fun thinking up their own names for the unusual rocks.

Traveling east on U.S. 26, turn north at Zigzag onto Lolo Pass Road (Road 18). Drive 0.4 mile, turn right onto gravel East Mountain Road, and continue 1.6 miles to the trailhead. There is room for only a few cars along the road here.

The hike begins as a pleasant walk through the woods on a narrow path crowded by tall bracken ferns, vine maple, and red huckleberry below tall Douglas firs. Cross an old road, climb a bit, level off, then begin climbing again in earnest.

After about 0.5 mile, the switchbacks end and the trail starts to follow a ridge. The ridge soon narrows, and the trail begins passing interesting rock formations. A spur trail on the left leads out to a rocky viewpoint, while the main trail continues around to the right. Another spur trail on the right leads a short distance along a more precipitous trail to a peekaboo hole in the rock overlooking a little rock spire; the view is neat but not worth the worry unless the group is small and children are careful.

Climb over a knob and your goal can be seen up to the left: a wall of rock. The trail skirts along the base of the rock wall to the right, switchbacks uphill, and ends alongside the rock formations. With care, follow footpaths out onto the promontories for eagle-eye views of the Zigzag River watershed.

10. Little Zigzag Falls

Type:	Dayhike
Difficulty:	Easy
Distance:	1 mile round-trip
Hikable:	Most of the year
Use:	Heavy
High point:	3200 feet
Elevation gain:	Negligible
Maps:	Green Trails—Government Camp; Mount Hood Wilderness

This is an ideal first hike for very young children on a visit to Mount Hood. It's just a few minutes' drive off U.S. 26, it's virtually level and not very long, and it ends at a lovely falls. Kids will enjoy wandering the easy path through the forest and playing by the pool at the base of the falls.

Traveling east on U.S. 26, drive 6 miles past Zigzag Ranger Station and turn left onto Road 2639. Drive 1.3 miles to the signed trailhead and

Little Zigzag Falls

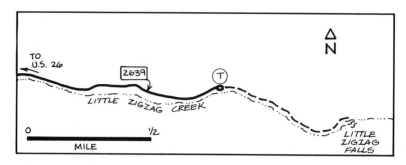

large parking turnout (the road is blocked to further travel at this point).

The well-constructed trail (completed in 1989) follows alongside icy, clear, swift Little Zigzag Creek, through a lush, narrow canyon. Listen closely to the sounds the creek makes as it tumbles over rocks and logs and flows along sandy shallows; you can almost hear it converse with itself in different voices. In early summer, skunk cabbage and rhododendrons are in bloom.

The base of Little Zigzag Falls is reached about 0.5 mile from the trailhead. Stand on the gambion—a structure built of rocks piled inside a cylinder of wire fencing—to watch the falls tumble about 75 feet in a series of short drops at the top, then one long cascade down an angled, mossy, chiseled rock face. The trail continues, making one switchback to climb to the top of the falls, where it ends.

11. Mirror Lake

Type:	Dayhike or backpack
Difficulty:	Moderate
Distance:	3.2 miles, loop
Hikable:	June through October
Use:	Heavy
High point:	4100 feet
Elevation gain:	700 feet
Maps:	Green Trails—Government Camp; Mount Hood Wilderness

This is one of the busiest trails on Mount Hood, for obvious reasons. It's relatively close to Portland and just the right length for a moderately easy hike, and the reward is a classic view of Mount Hood towering above

Mirror Lake. Even on a weekday, you probably won't be alone; so take particular care to have as little impact as possible, by staying on the trail, keeping voices low at the lake, and scrupulously picking up after yourself. Early summer is a wonderful time for this hike, when the rhododendrons and beargrass are in bloom.

From Government Camp, drive 2 miles west on U.S. 26 to the trailhead on the south side of the highway. Cross Camp Creek on a footbridge and start up the trail, which immediately passes several big tree stumps with springboard cuts, evidence of old-time logging.

Walk through Douglas fir, cedar, and pine forest for the first 0.5 mile, then cross a scree slope that seems to house a colony of little, furry pikas (listen for their call). Back in the woods, look for more springboard-cut stumps while switchbacking up toward the lake. Ask children to look for faces in some of the old, notched stumps; one in particular has evolved into an Old Man of the Mountain as time has sculpted features from natural and humanmade blemishes. The far-off sound of eighteen-wheelers grinding up the highway accompanies hikers most of the way along the trail, virtually until the trail drops into the lake basin.

At 1.4 miles, you'll meet the lake's gurgling outlet creek on the left and a trail junction, the start of a 0.4-mile loop trail around the lake. A sign indicates that campsites are to the right, and that's also the fastest route to the best lakeside picnic sites. The right fork arrives at the lake in a couple of minutes.

Rough stairs lead to nice picnic sites on this side of the lake. A short

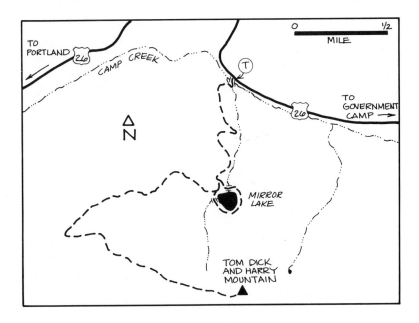

Mount Hood from Mirror Lake

distance farther, the trail splits. The left fork continues around the lake, granting postcard views of Mount Hood. It follows a log boardwalk across the lake's boggy inlet and continues to the trail junction near its outlet.

The right fork leads steadily up another 1.6 miles (and 800 feet in elevation) to the top of Tom Dick and Harry Mountain, a worthwhile extension of the hike for older children after a pause at the lake. The trail here is less used and hence a bit rougher. Carry binoculars and keep looking upward, especially around the cliffs near the top of the mountain. In August 1990, a nesting pair of peregrine falcons was introduced here.

12. Umbrella Falls–Sahalie Falls Loop

Type: Dayhike
Difficulty: Moderate
Distance: 4.1 miles, loop
Hikable: June through October
Use: Light
High point: 5240 feet
Elevation gain: 800 feet
Maps: Green Trails—Mt. Hood;
Mount Hood Wilderness

Summer hikes don't get much better than this. Early in the season the trail is lined with pale-green huckleberry leaves and white bear-grass plumes; later the meadows are ablaze with wildflowers. Just about when the flower show starts to fade, the huckleberries come on with a vengeance, and what child can resist berry-picking? Then there are the

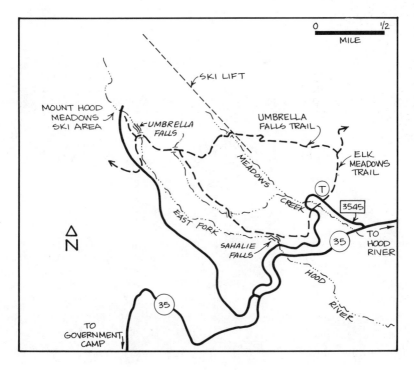

waterfalls and the views. The novelty of hiking across Mount Hood
Meadows' ski runs is titillating for children who ski here in the winter.
There are various ways to hike part or all of the trails around Hood River
Meadows; this loop route makes a good, varied, moderate dayhike for
families.

From Government Camp, follow U.S. 26 east about 3 miles to the
junction with State 35. Follow State 35 east about 7 miles and turn left
at the sign to Hood River Meadows on Road 3545 (about a mile east of
the turn-off to Mount Hood Meadows ski area). Drive 0.4 mile and park
in a turnout at the trailhead for Sahalie Falls Trail, on the left side of
the road.

With all the huckleberries at the trailhead, it may be hard to get
a group started up the trail in late August or early September; assure
them there's a lot more ahead. The trail crosses a boggy area on a log,

Bridge crossing East Fork Hood River below Umbrella Falls

then leads to a creek that is crossed on rocks. Follow the creek up to a road, cross it, then continue up to Sahalie Falls, off the main trail to the left at 0.5 mile.

Back on the main trail, climb uphill steadily, following the East Fork Hood River's east bank. At about 1 mile, descend momentarily to cross a creek, then resume the climb, passing more little creeks and traversing some meadows. At 1.7 miles, the trail reaches a T junction with Umbrella Falls Trail. Turn left and walk 0.3 mile to Umbrella Falls, also on the East Fork Hood River.

The exceptionally pretty falls is a great destination for lunch or just playtime. A bridge crosses the wide, sandy creek below the falls, which streams gently down a rounded rock face like rain down an umbrella. An asphalt path leads 0.2 mile to the top of the falls; continue a few steps farther to reach the lower end of the Mount Hood Meadows parking area.

To resume the hike from Umbrella Falls, return 0.3 mile to the junction and continue straight. About 0.2 mile from the junction the trail emerges from the forest and begins traversing a wide meadow with a great view of the mountain—it's a ski run. The trail passes under a ski lift and continues in and out of forest and meadow for about a mile before reentering the forest for good. After about 0.2 mile in the woods, bear right at the three-way junction with Elk Meadows Trail. Continue another 0.4 mile back to the trailhead.

13. Tamawanas Falls

Type:	Dayhike
Difficulty:	Moderate
Distance:	4.2 miles round-trip
Hikable:	May through October
Use:	Heavy
High point:	3400 feet
Elevation gain:	360 feet
Maps:	Green Trails—Mt. Hood; Mount Hood Wilderness

Four wooden footbridges that *surely* shelter trolls, a butterfly-shaped waterfall, a steep talus slope: this trail packs a whole lot of interest per mile. It's rated moderate because of distance and elevation gain, but all the trailside attractions (and the anticipation of more) make the trip speed by.

From Hood River, drive south on State 35 about 25 miles and pull over at the sign to East Fork Trail, on the west side of the road. From Government Camp, follow U.S. 26 east about 3 miles to the junction with State 35. Follow State 35 east and north about 14 miles to the trailhead, which is just north of Sherwood Campground.

Walk through the campground toward milky-colored East Fork Hood River and cross it on a narrow log bridge. Two-tier railings make the bridge relatively safe for children, but you'll want to watch them closely just the same. At the end of the bridge, bear right. The trail heads north for a rather unappealing 0.6 mile, following above the river and in sight of the highway. It then bears left and meets a trail junction (go straight), and things improve quickly. The trail drops into the cool canyon of Cold Spring Creek, crosses the creek, and heads up the noisy, moss-banked stream. Encourage the kids to get down on their knees to examine tiny bunchberry and twinflower blossoms, or their berries later in the season.

Continue upstream on the rather rocky trail, rounding a big boulder at about 1.5 miles. Walk along the bottom of a scree slope past a junction with Trail 650B, then recross the creek on a log bridge. Switchback up the canyon a couple of times, drop down some steps, and cross the creek for the last time. From there, it's about 0.25 mile up some switchbacks and around the hill to a view of Tamawanas Falls at the trail's end.

The falls drop about 100 feet through a depression worn in a cliff of columnar basalt. Cliffs fan out like butterfly wings on either side of the stream of water.

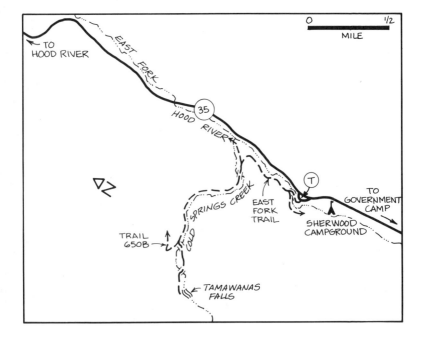

Cold Spring Creek

14. Cloud Cap Loop

Type: Dayhike
Difficulty: Moderate
Distance: 3 miles, loop
Hikable: July through September
Use: Light
High point: 6640 feet
Elevation gain: 920 feet
Maps: Green Trails—Mt. Hood;
Mount Hood Wilderness

The Timberline Trail encircling Mount Hood offers panoramic alpine backpacking, but opportunities for short dayhikes on it are few, as road access is limited. Probably the most-hiked sections are those heading east and west from Timberline Lodge. The Cloud Cap Loop isn't as crowded, and it includes 1.4 miles of the 40.7-mile round-the-mountain trail as well as an opportunity to stop by a grand old mountain chateau. This high on the mountain, don't be too casual about hike preparations; carry sunglasses and sunscreen as well as extra clothes to wear in case of sudden weather changes.

 From Government Camp, follow U.S. 26 and State 35 east and north 19 miles to Cooper Spur Road and turn west. From Hood River, the turnoff is about 24 miles south on State 35. Continue 2.4 miles and turn left at the sign to Tilly Jane Recreation Area. In 1.4 miles, bear right onto gravel Road 3512 and follow the washboardlike road 8.4 miles to the turnoff to Tilly Jane Campground, on the left. Look for the trailhead at the end of the road.

Walk this loop clockwise to get the least-interesting climbing out of the way at the beginning. Head west, following signs for Trail 600A, down to cross a creek, then up past an amphitheater and into the trees. This trail offers a good opportunity to practice pacing; it's a pretty steady uphill climb. At about 0.5 mile the trail follows along the edge of a gaping sandy canyon, at the bottom of which trickles the headwaters of Polallie Creek.

At about 1 mile the trail breaks out of the trees and enters an alpine rock garden with a view of Mount Hood's summit straight ahead. Continue up another 0.2 mile to the junction with Timberline Trail. After a little R&R, your party may want to continue straight up the trail onto Cooper Spur for some high-mountain exploration. Otherwise, turn right on Timberline Trail to continue the loop.

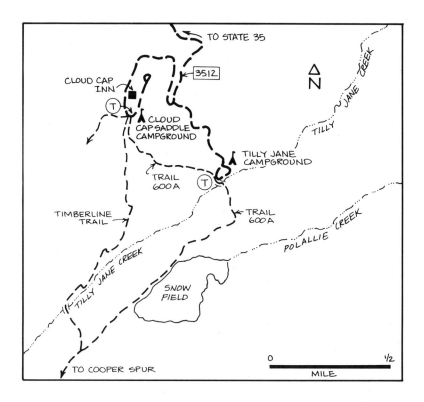

From the junction, the trail starts dropping gradually through a dazzling show of alpine wildflowers that peaks in August. Much of the way it follows the pretty beginnings of Tilly Jane Creek as it trickles through the rocky alpine landscape. After about 1 mile the trail reaches timberline again; continue about 0.4 mile to the road.

Cloud Cap Inn, built in 1889, is just up the road a short walk. It was originally built as a private mountain retreat; currently it's used by the Crag Rats, a Hood River climbing club, as a base for climbs and mountain rescues. Unless some Crag Rats happen to be there, you'll have to enjoy it from the porch.

Pick up Tilly Jane Trail (600A) and head east 0.5 mile, dropping gently through the subalpine forest and crossing a few tiny creeks before reaching the parking area.

Clackamas and Molalla Rivers

State 211 and 224

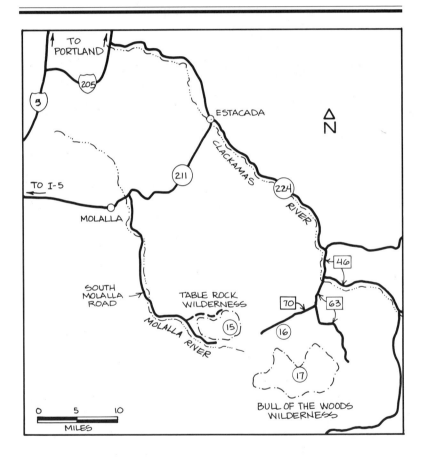

15. Table Rock

Type: Dayhike
Difficulty: Difficult
Distance: 5.4 miles round-trip
Hikable: June through October
Use: Light
High point: 4880 feet
Elevation gain: 1255 feet
Maps: USGS Rooster Rock;
BLM Table Rock Wilderness

This Table Rock is the centerpiece of a pocket Bureau of Land Management (BLM) wilderness area southeast of Portland. The main trail to the summit is a good choice if children are ready for a challenge and if adults are ready to explore some new territory. Vistas are dramatic, and the plant life is varied and unusual; wildflowers bloom profusely on the upper slopes in July, and the collection of trees found on the summit constitutes a mini-arboretum in itself. There's virtually no water along the trail, so backpacking isn't an option; but the flat summit lends itself

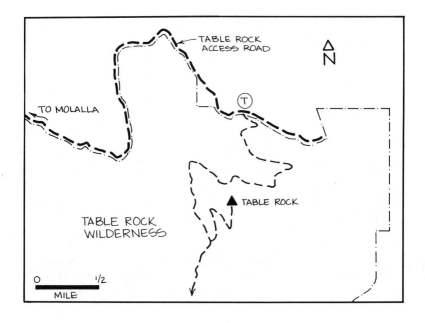

Approaching summit of Table Rock

well to picnics. After your hike, stop for a swim in one of the many swimming holes along the Molalla River.

The trailhead is 28.7 miles southeast of Molalla on mostly paved roads. Signage on the way to the trailhead is sparse. BLM officials say they want to avoid promoting the area to minimize damage to ecologically sensitive areas, and those signs that have been posted tend to get vandalized quickly; so follow these road directions carefully.

From State 211 in Molalla, turn south at the east end of town onto South Mathias Road. In 0.3 mile, turn left onto South Feyrer Park Road. Continue 1.7 miles, cross the river, and turn right on South Dickey Prairie Road. In 5.3 miles, turn right across the Molalla River, then in 0.3 mile bear left, following the paved road (South Molalla Road). In 12.7 miles, just before a bridge, bear left onto gravel Middle Fork Road. In 2.6 miles, turn right onto Table Rock Access Road and continue 5.8 miles to the trailhead, marked with a small sign on the right.

Immediately, the trail starts up into a gorgeous forest that appears to have been selectively logged many years ago—a stark contrast to the clearcuts that can be seen through the trees. This wilderness area is a forested island in a sea of clearcuts, as can be seen from the road and again from the summit. For the first mile, the trail ascends steadily through tall Douglas firs, rhododendrons, and beargrass, making a few long switchbacks. At about 1.2 miles, it emerges from the forest to start across a 0.4-mile-wide scree slope below a sheer wall of columnar basalt. The trail there is narrow, rocky, and brushy in places; urge children to take care with their footing.

Reenter the forest, again ascending steadily. At 2.1 miles, climb up onto a saddle; bear left. A false summit is reached at 2.5 miles; then climb up onto the real summit at 2.7 miles. Children are safe as long as they don't tempt fate too close to the edge of the mountain's wide, flat top. On a clear day Mount Hood, Mount Jefferson, and the Three Sisters can be seen. Bagby Hot Springs (Hike 16) is only about 7 miles east of here, but there are currently no trail links between Table Rock and Mount Hood National Forest.

16. Bagby Hot Springs

Type:	Dayhike or backpack
Difficulty:	Easy
Distance:	3 miles round-trip
Hikable:	Most of the year
Use:	Heavy
High point:	2272 feet
Elevation gain:	190 feet
Maps:	USGS Bagby Hot Springs;
	Mount Hood National Forest

Big wood-stave tubs and narrow baths carved of single logs capture the sulphur-scented hot water that bubbles out of the ground near the Hot Springs Fork of the Collawash River—a welcome treat, especially

Snacktime outside bathhouse at Bagby Hot Springs

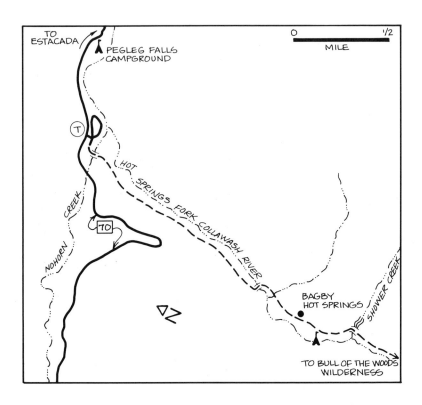

when hiking in the cool of late fall or early spring (or even midwinter, if snowpack permits). Bagby is a "clothing optional" spot; some visitors bathe with swimsuits, others in the buff. Hikers uncomfortable with public nudity might consider choosing another hike. Otherwise, Bagby is great fun with kids. They'll enjoy exploring the hot and cold springs, the old guard station, and the bathing facilities. The water emerges at 136° F; prime the tub with a few buckets of cold water first. Bagby is always crowded on weekends and often on weekdays as well; the best bet is to go on a weekday first thing in the morning, preferably in spring or fall.

From Estacada, follow State 224 southeast 26 miles to Ripplebrook Ranger Station. Continue 0.5 mile past the ranger station and bear right onto Forest Road 46. In 3.6 miles, turn right onto Forest Road 63. In another 3.6 miles, turn right onto Forest Road 70. Continue 6 miles to the large trailhead parking area, on the left.

From the trailhead, follow an asphalt path 30 yards to a long log bridge over Nohorn Creek. After the bridge, the trail becomes a wide dirt path, level or gently ascending through old-growth forest. At about 0.6 mile the trail meets and follows alongside the Hot Springs Fork of the Collawash River. Plank boardwalks or raised trail sections help hikers over boggy spots here and there.

At 1.25 miles the trail crosses the Hot Springs Fork on another tall, skinny bridge at a dramatic point where a huge boulder splits the river into two chutes. From there, the trail steepens somewhat for the final 0.25 mile to the springs and main bathhouse, on the left.

Some tubs are in enclosed bathhouses; others are open to the woods and other bathers. You may have to wait your turn for a tub. Up the trail and off to the left a bit (beyond the old guard station) is another tub and, near it, a bubbling hot spring that feeds it; kids will enjoy exploring here (the spring feeding the main bathhouse is fenced off).

Overnight camping is not permitted right at the springs; rather, camp 0.3 mile up the trail along the river at Shower Creek. Dayhikers may enjoy extending their visit with a walk to the falls at Shower Creek or farther; the trail enters Bull of the Woods Wilderness 0.6 mile beyond Bagby and continues in deep forest, crossing a series of creeks, to Silver Creek Lake, a total of 7.3 miles.

17. Pansy Lake

Type:	Dayhike or backpack
Difficulty:	Easy
Distance:	2.6 miles round-trip
Hikable:	June through October
Use:	Heavy
High point:	3994 feet
Elevation gain:	450 feet
Maps:	USGS Bull of the Woods;
	Mount Hood National Forest

The hike to Pansy Lake is perhaps a little tougher than that to Bagby—steeper, though shorter—and a lot less crowded; rangers classify it as medium to heavy use, as opposed to Bagby's extra-heavy. There are campsites at the lake, but equally appealing for overnighting is Pansy Basin, a short detour on an unmaintained spur off the lake trail. The prolific beargrass bloom along the trail usually reaches its peak in late June.

Follow road directions for Bagby Hot Springs (Hike 16) to the junction of Roads 46 and 63. From there, drive 5.7 miles up Road 63 (passing the turn-off to Bagby) and turn right on Road 6340. Drive 8 miles, then bear right on Road 6341; continue 3.6 miles to a wide turnout on the right and park. (If there is no trail sign, look for a sign indicating the end of road maintenance.) The trail starts across the road to the right of a small creek.

Immediately the trail passes a sign indicating the start of Bull of the Woods Wilderness. The trail climbs steadily most of the way through deep

Log "bridges" across Pansy Lake outlet

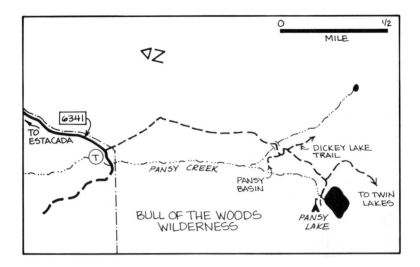

forest, crossing first a small stream and then a larger one, both on steppingstones. At 0.9 mile, an unsigned spur trail on the right leads downhill a short distance to Pansy Basin, an open, grassy meadow inviting for young backpackers.

Just up the main trail, pass a junction with the Dickey Lake Trail, on the left. At 1.2 miles, the trail levels off at a fork, with the trail to Twin Lakes heading left and Pansy Lake a hop, skip, and a jump to the right.

Follow the lake spur along the water's edge, passing a small campsite and crossing the lake's outlet creek on a narrow log. There's a larger campsite and a pleasant little beach just beyond the creek, where the trail ends.

North Santiam River

State 22

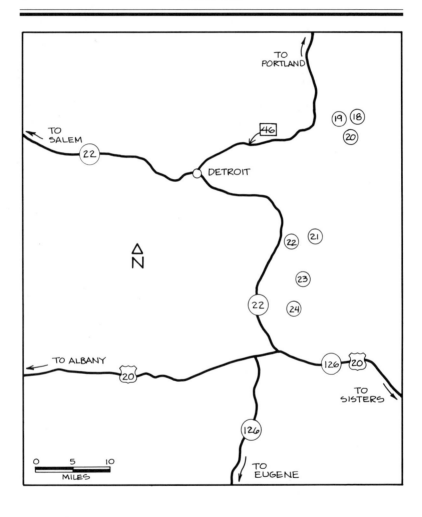

Olallie Butte beyond Russ Lake

18. Russ Lake

Type: Dayhike or backpack
Difficulty: Easy
Distance: 1.6 miles round-trip
Hikable: June through September
Use: Light
High point: 4600 feet
Elevation gain: 100 feet
Maps: Green Trails—Breitenbush;
Mount Hood National Forest

Most Willamette Valley residents would consider the Olallie Lakes Scenic Area too far a drive for a day trip. Instead, make it a destination for a weekend or week of high-mountain hiking and boating. Take along a canoe, or rent a rowboat at Olallie Lake Resort. No motorboats are permitted, adding to the pristine magic of the area. Many of the lakes are air-stocked every year; fishing is best in June and September. For hiking, choose between a dozen or so dayhike routes. Russ Lake is one of just three options included in this book; for more ideas, scan the map or pick up trail guides at Mount Hood National Forest headquarters or ranger stations.

The trail to Russ Lake is a good warm-up. It passes three lakes, though it intersects other trails, creating options for extending a hike. All three lakes have good fishing; a tribal permit is required (available from the Warm Springs Indian Reservation) to fish on Jude or Russ lakes.

From Salem, take State 22 east to Detroit. Turn north onto Forest Road 46 at the sign to Breitenbush. Continue 23.7 miles to Road 4690 and turn right. (From Portland, take State 211 to Estacada, then follow State 242 for 26 miles to Ripplebrook Ranger Station. Turn south on

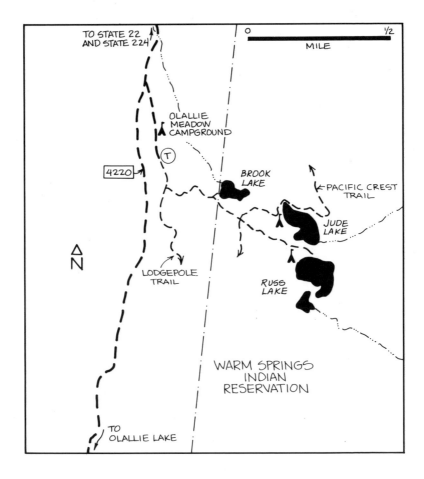

Forest Road 46 and follow it for 25 miles to Road 4690.) Take Road 4690 (turns to gravel in 7.7 miles) south 8.2 miles, turn right onto Skyline Road (Road 4220), drive 1.4 miles, and turn left at Olallie Meadow Campground. Park at the trailhead parking area at the end of the campground.

The trail starts at the edge of lovely, broad Olallie Meadow and heads immediately into the trees on a narrow path lined with beargrass and huckleberry. At 0.2 mile, turn left at the junction with Lodgepole Trail. Soon the trail starts to climb gently; at 0.4 mile, a spur to the left leads a short distance up to charming little Brook Lake.

Continuing up the main trail, it reaches the junction with the Pacific Crest Trail at 0.5 mile; for a side trip to Jude Lake, turn left onto the PCT and walk 0.2 mile to the lake's northwest corner. Jude Lake is another charmer, with a campsite near the shore (a sign points the way). Back on the main trail, it's another 0.3 mile to Russ Lake, passing the southeast end of Jude Lake along the way. Russ Lake is big and green and round—definitely the prize on this hike. Olallie Butte looms across the water. For true luxury, pack in a small raft and spend the day floating and trolling.

If the kids like this hike and are ready for more of the same, try the similar, but more challenging, Red Lakes Trail. It starts just south of Olallie Guard Station, hits Top Lake at 1.3 miles, Sheep Lake at 2.8 miles, and three more lakes spaced no more than 0.5 mile apart.

19. Fish Lake

Type:	Dayhike or backpack
Difficulty:	Moderate
Distance:	3.2 miles round-trip
Hikable:	June through September
Use:	Heavy
High point:	4900 feet
Elevation gain:	420 feet
Maps:	Green Trails—Breitenbush;
	Mount Hood National Forest

There are trailheads at either end of Fish Lake Trail, but the dramatic approach to Fish Lake from the south is an argument for starting at the southern trailhead. Besides, this trailhead is closer for families camping in the area. You could make this a one-way, downhill, 2.8-mile hike, but the long car shuttle required makes it hard to justify.

Fish Lake

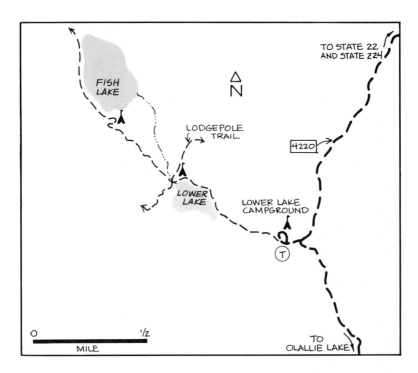

For road directions to Olallie Lakes Scenic Area, see Hike 18, Russ Lake. From the turn-off to Olallie Meadow Campground, continue south on Skyline Road (Road 4220) another 3.1 miles and turn right at the sign to Lower Lake Campground.

From the trailhead, the trail starts out level, then descends gently to reach Lower Lake at 0.3 mile. Follow along the lakeshore, passing a nice little gravel beach. The bank is sharp, but there are plenty of appealing places to pause for a snack or some rock-throwing. At 0.6 mile, the trail passes a pleasant campsite at a shallow cove at the lake's far end.

Cross the lake's outlet creek and go straight across the junction with Lodgepole Trail. There the trail starts dropping, through a jungle of beargrass and huckleberry, to reach a magnificent view of Fish Lake, nearly 200 feet below, at 1 mile. Kids may have second thoughts about hiking down that far (knowing they'll eventually have to hike back up), but reassure them that it's not really all that far, that switchbacks make the grade pretty moderate, and that they can take their time on the return. Begin the plunge down to the lake, through an old-growth forest, down four switchbacks and hopping across a creek on midstream rocks, to reach the pretty lakeshore at 1.6 miles. There's an appealing campsite near the lake, and trout fishing is usually good in June and September.

20. Monon Lake

Type:	Dayhike or backpack
Difficulty:	Easy
Distance:	3.8 miles, loop
Hikable:	June through September
Use:	Heavy
High point:	4960 feet
Elevation gain:	Negligible
Maps:	Green Trails—Breitenbush;
	Mount Hood National Forest

Unlike long forest trails, paths around lakes really let you see where you're going and where you've been—a fun proposition for kids. It's possible to hike all the way around either Olallie or Monon Lake, but

Monon Lake

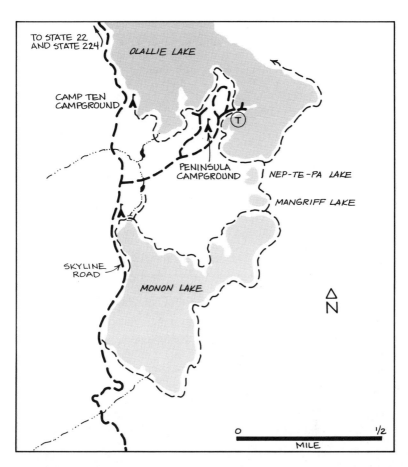

the trail around Monon is more remote. Also, swimming is permitted in Monon Lake, but not in Olallie, as it's a drinking water source. Really ambitious hikers can hike around both (6 miles total).

For road directions to Olallie Lakes Scenic Area, see Hike 18, Russ Lake. From the turn-off to Olallie Meadow Campground, continue south on Skyline Road another 5 miles, passing Olallie Guard Station on the left, and turn left at the sign to Peninsula Campground. Follow signs to the boat ramp.

The trail passes the campground and follows along the Olallie lakeshore. At 0.4 mile bear right onto Monon—Olallie Trail and follow it past tiny Nep-Te-Pa Lake and then another tiny, steep-banked lake, Mangriff. At 0.6 mile the trail reaches the start of the Monon Lake loop trail.

Walking counterclockwise, you can see Mount Jefferson across Monon Lake and may even surprise a family of mergansers or other birds on the lake. Here the lakeshore is a series of deep bays, so only a small portion of it can be seen at a time. After passing a small campsite 0.4 mile from the start of the loop, the trail leaves the deeper bays and permits a view across the lake itself. At 0.6 mile a spur leads to another little lake, with Olallie Butte rising behind it. Cross a creek on a footbridge, then pass the first of several small campsites at 0.8 mile.

Here the trail is squeezed between Monon Lake and Road 4220; in fact, at 0.9 mile, the trail runs up onto the road for 0.2 mile until it resumes, veering off the road and back toward the lake. At 1.5 miles a boardwalk and series of little plank bridges lead over a swampy area. Pass another little campsite at 2.5 miles, then head up the only significant incline on the trail (it's steep but short). When Mount Jefferson can be seen again, you're almost back to the start of the loop. Walk back past Nep-Te-Pa Lake and Olallie's southwest shore to the starting point.

21. Pamelia Lake

Type:	Dayhike (backpacking not recommended)
Difficulty:	Moderate
Distance:	4.4 miles round-trip
Hikable:	June through October
Use:	Heavy
High point:	3920 feet
Elevation gain:	800 feet
Maps:	Green Trails—Mt. Jefferson; Mount Hood National Forest

The trail to Pamelia Lake follows a lovely creek slipping through a venerable old-growth forest and ends at a large mountain lake – no wonder it's so popular. Before making plans to go to Pamelia Lake, check in with the Detroit Ranger Station; beginning in 1992, the Forest Service plans to require permits for both dayhiking and backpacking in this area, and there will be a limited number issued. The lake's level drops over the summer, and the lake is most attractive in early July, when rhododendrons bloom, through August, though less crowded in September.

From Detroit, drive 12.5 miles south on State 22 and turn east on Pamelia Road (Forest Road 2246). Follow the road (paved until mile 2.9) 3.8 miles to the trailhead at the road's end.

The trail begins as a wide, gently ascending path through a forest.

Pamelia Lake

A few minutes from the trailhead a sign indicates that you're entering Mount Jefferson Wilderness. Continue walking alongside rushing Pamelia Creek, lined with moss-draped, round rocks.

The scene doesn't change much until about 1.9 miles, when something seems different—the creek is gone! It's still within earshot at first, but over the final 0.3 mile to the lake it fades from hearing as well, and all you'll hear are bird calls and your own footfalls. Just beyond a trail junction at 2.2 miles lies Pamelia Lake. There are plenty of campsites, but consider camping elsewhere to avoid using an already overused area.

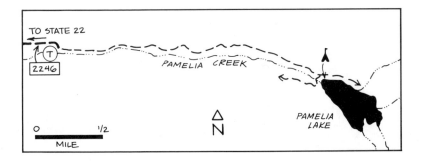

22. Independence Rock

Type: Dayhike
Difficulty: Easy to moderate
Distance: 2.2 miles, loop
Hikable: April through November
Use: Light
High point: 2840 feet
Elevation gain: 390 feet
Maps: Green Trails—Mt. Jefferson;
Mount Hood National Forest

The big attraction of Independence Rock isn't the view from the top but the tiny ants that build fantastic anthills, taller than many children, all along the lower half of the trail. The Latin name of the ant that lives here is *Formica formica,* with the accent on the first syllable (not like the counter top). Most visitors know instinctively not to disturb these natural wonders, but if the children in your party are destruction-prone, a word of restraint might be in order. This hike makes a great halfway-point break on the way from Salem to Bend.

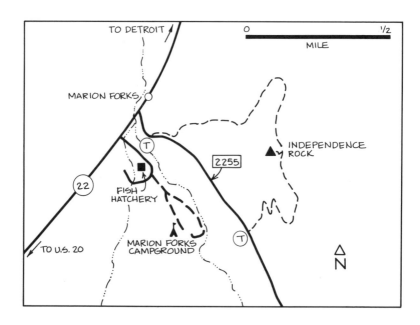

Anthill beside Independence Rock Trail

From Detroit, follow State 22 south 16.6 miles to the community of Marion Forks. The trail starts just 0.1 mile up Road 2255, on the left. Parking may be a problem; if permitted, park in the large lot across the road from Marion Forks Restaurant. Otherwise, you may have to park at the fish hatchery or Marion Forks Campground, both just across Marion Creek, and walk back along the road.

The trail starts level, heads up a hill, then levels off again at about 0.2 mile. Here's where to start looking for anthills, some right along the trail and others several yards away; the ants seem to prefer this particular elevation. The mounds may be as tall as 4 feet; they consist of dry fir needles and quarter-inch-long ants swarming over them, depositing and rearranging the needles.

At 0.4 mile the trail starts to climb again at a nice, steady grade, away from Antland. The woods are pretty, with old growth Douglas fir and rhododendrons. At 1 mile the trail reaches the spur trail up Independence Rock, just ahead. A trail has been hacked out of this tall outcrop leading to the summit; it's a trail, not a scramble, but watch children

carefully just the same. It's fun sitting on top of the rock, but the view features no mountains: just forests, clearcuts, two neat little houses, and a neat lawn to the west (that's the fish hatchery on Marion Creek). You can't see the North Santiam River, but you can hear its roar.

To return, retrace your steps or continue on the main trail, which drops down a few switchbacks 0.7 mile to Road 2255, at a point 0.5 mile up from the lower trailhead you started on. Unless there's logging above, the road is pretty safe to walk alongside, and a loop is always an interesting alternative. But there are few if any anthills on this return leg, and it may be more fun coming and going on the same trail (2 miles round-trip).

23. Marion Lake

Type:	Dayhike (backpacking not recommended)
Difficulty:	Moderate
Distance:	5.4 miles, loop
Hikable:	June through September
Use:	Heavy
High point:	4170 feet
Elevation gain:	510 feet
Maps:	Green Trails—Mt. Jefferson; Mount Hood National Forest

An exceptionally beautiful lake and an interesting route getting there are what make this hike so appealing. Like Pamelia Lake Trail (Hike 21), this trail may be subject to a limited-access permit system for both dayhikers and backpackers beginning in 1992. Overnight camping at

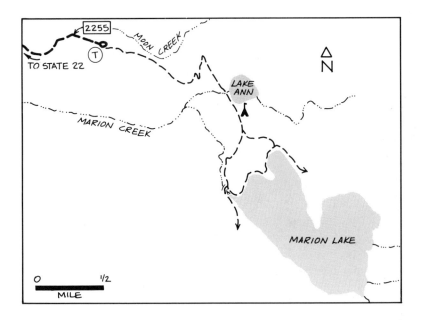

Marion Lake is limited. There are some nice campsites at Lake Ann, along the way. Better yet, pack a picnic and plan to spend the day strolling in, exploring the lake area, and wandering back out, camping elsewhere. It's more fun without a heavy pack anyway.

From Detroit, drive south on State 22 for 16.6 miles and turn left onto Road 2255 (gravel after 0.7 mile). Continue 4.6 miles to the trailhead at the end of the road.

The wide trail follows a rolling, uphill grade most of the way. At about 0.4 mile the sound of Moon Creek can be heard, off to the left but out of sight. By 0.8 mile the sound has gone, replaced by the gurgle of little nearby springs. At about 1 mile the trail steepens. Step across a small creek, then at 1.5 miles meet Lake Ann's outlet creek. Walk a short distance through a corridor of vine maple (brilliant in late September) and cross a jumble of rocks at the end of the lake; listen to the creek rumbling and singing underfoot.

Lake Ann is lovely, but its banks are either steep or marshy, not appealing for picnicking. Continue up the trail along the lakeshore, passing campsites at the lake's east end. A junction at 1.8 miles signals the start of the loop trail at Marion Lake's north end. Going clockwise, pass a scree slope and reach the lake and another trail fork in 0.3 mile.

Bearing right, walk along a well-trampled slope above the land until the trail resumes in about 0.2 mile, following around and above the lake. The trail switches back once to ascend a peninsula, then drops down to a gorgeous, substantial footbridge across the lake's outlet 1 mile from

Marion Lake

the start of the loop. Rather than cross the footbridge, bear right down the trail above the outlet creek that drops down to the start of the loop in 0.8 mile. From there, bear left and continue back to the trailhead on the main trail.

24. Pika–Fir Lakes

Type:	Dayhike or backpack
Difficulty:	Easy
Distance:	1.8 miles round-trip
Hikable:	June through September
Use:	Light
High point:	4050 feet
Elevation gain:	180 feet
Maps:	Green Trails—Mt. Jefferson; Mount Hood National Forest

In contrast to popular, dazzling Marion Lake, Pika–Fir Trail is rather underwhelming to adults—and may seem just delightful to kids. It's lightly used, and the two lakes it accesses are small but closely spaced. Carry fishing gear; fishing is best in June and September. The best camping is at Fir Lake. The area is boggy; be prepared for mosquitoes, especially in June and July.

From Detroit, take State 22 south for about 26 miles. Just south of where the highway crosses the North Santiam River, turn east on Road 2267 (Big Meadows Road). Drive 1 mile and turn left onto Road 2257. Go 1.7 miles and turn right at the junction, still on Road 2257 (now gravel). Drive another 0.7 mile, passing Fay Lake, to reach the trailhead, on the right.

The trail heads gently up for the first 0.2 mile, drops a bit, then heads back up to pass Pika Lake at 0.5 mile. The lake is nice, but not the main

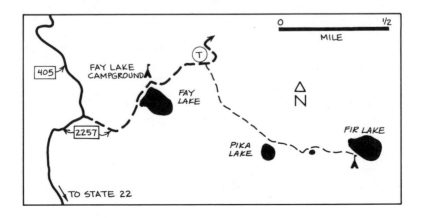

attraction; look for water lilies along the shore. Continue up the trail, passing an unnamed mudhole at 0.7 mile. The trail drops again just before reaching Fir Lake, which is much more appealing than Pika, with campsites to boot. The shoreline is pretty; explorers in your party can walk all the way around the lake.

Fir Lake

South Santiam River

U.S. 20

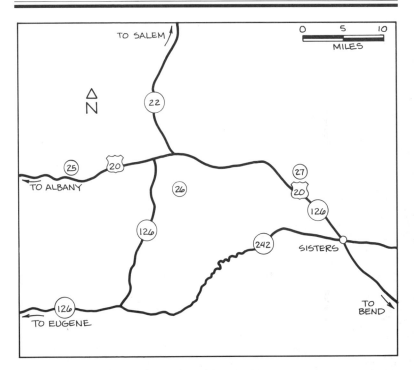

TO SALEM

0   5   10
MILES

N

22

25   20
TO ALBANY

26

27
20
126

126

242   SISTERS

126
TO EUGENE

TO BEND

Lookout on Sand Mountain

25. Iron Mountain

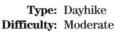

Type:	Dayhike
Difficulty:	Moderate
Distance:	3.6 miles round-trip
Hikable:	June through October
Use:	Heavy
High point:	5455 feet
Elevation gain:	1385 feet
Maps:	USGS Harter Mountain;
	Willamette National Forest

The trail up Iron Mountain would seem a tougher climb if it weren't surrounded by a blaze of wildflowers at every step and if the goal weren't a Forest Service fire lookout. This is a favorite July wildflower trek among many Oregon hikers, and children enjoy the chance to poke around the lookout, perhaps getting a lesson in fire-finding from the ranger on guard.

From the junction of Santiam Highway (U.S. 20) and State 126, head west on Santiam Highway 9 miles and turn south on Road 15 to a small trailhead sign (at milepost 63). Continue 0.2 mile to a large parking area.

From the parking area, the trail cuts back through the woods, crosses the highway at 0.2 mile, and begins its climb with a gentle ascent through a deep, airy forest of old-growth Douglas fir. At about 0.8 mile the forest starts to open up somewhat, and at 1 mile a trail junction is reached; bear right. In another 0.2 mile bear right again at the junction with Cone Peak Trail.

From the junction, the trail is exposed (hot in summer) and rather

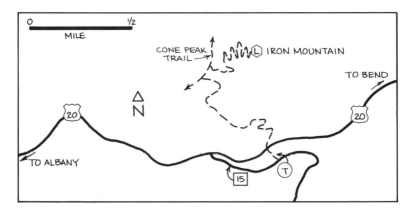

Mount Jefferson from summit of Iron Mountain

steep. The consolation is the open fields of wildflowers blooming profusely in midsummer. Take time with children on this last 0.7 mile to the lookout, snooping at the flowers and enjoying the view opening up as the trail ascends.

The summit isn't much more than a rocky knob, without room for much more than a lookout. Watch children carefully up here; it's safe enough if they don't start clambering down the rocks. Walk around the catwalk to take in the view of Mount Hood, Mount Jefferson, Mount Washington, the Three Sisters, and the tiptop of Three-Fingered Jack. Encourage children to sign the hikers' register; they may enjoy leafing through it to scan the hometowns of hikers that preceded them.

26. Sand Mountain

Type:	Dayhike
Difficulty:	Easy
Distance:	1.25 miles, loop
Hikable:	June through October
Use:	Light
High point:	5459 feet
Elevation gain:	340 feet
Maps:	USGS Santiam Junction;
	Willamette National Forest

The hike around the rim of the crater is just one part of what's sure to be a memorable family outing to Sand Mountain, located southwest of Hoodoo Ski Bowl. This cinder cone is the centerpiece of the Sand Mountain Geologic Special Interest Area, which was established in the

Sand Mountain Lookout, with Mount Washington beyond

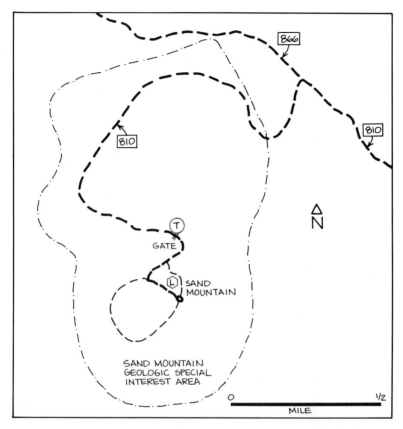

late 1980s to protect it and neighboring cinder cones from off-road vehicle damage. But what children will probably find most interesting is the lookout cabin on the crater rim. Though it appears to have been there for years, it's actually a reconstructed cabin from Whiskey Peak in southern Oregon. It was reassembled (with windows from another lookout and a fire-finder from yet another) on the rim in 1989 and 1990. Visitors are welcome on the catwalk and inside to look through the fire-finder and talk with the ranger about life on Sand Mountain.

From the junction of State 22 and U.S. 20/State 126, drive east 5.5 miles and turn south at the sign to Hoodoo Ski Bowl (Road 2690). Continue 3.2 miles, following signs to Big Lake, and bear right onto dirt Road 810. Stay on this road for 4.5 miles until it ends at a gate. Spur roads might make route-finding a bit challenging. The following tips should help: 1.5 miles from the start of Road 810, bear right; at 2.5 miles, go straight; at 2.9 miles, turn left. Park where the road ends at the gate.

From the gate, walk up the road 0.1 mile, then veer off the road onto a footpath. It's a steep, short route to the lookout at the summit, at 0.3

mile. Plan to spend some time visiting with the ranger and admiring the views of Hoodoo Ski Bowl, Black Butte, Big Lake, Mount Washington, the Three Sisters, and Mount Hood on very clear days.

To continue the hike, walk down the barren, sandy summit to the fenced turnaround at the end of the road and cross it (through narrow openings in the fence). The trail drops down, steeply at first, to circumnavigate the crater. Though the rim trail isn't narrow enough to be dangerous, children will look in awe into the small, steep-walled crater and down the outside of the cinder cone. The trail levels out, then climbs rather steeply before meeting the road. Follow the road back down past the gate to your car.

27. Black Butte

Type:	Dayhike
Difficulty:	Moderate
Distance:	4 miles round-trip
Hikable:	June through October
Use:	Heavy
High point:	6436 feet
Elevation gain:	1556 feet
Maps:	USGS Black Butte;
	Deschutes National Forest

Gazing out from Black Butte Ranch resort, or driving by on the highway, the tall, black, symmetrical cinder cone of Black Butte looks like something you'd want to climb. The road goes most of the way up; 2 miles of hiking finishes the ascent. On top is a veritable living museum of lookout towers, adding to the uniqueness of this hike.

From the junction of State 22 and U.S. 20/State 126, drive east 20 miles and turn north on Indian Ford Road. In 0.2 mile, bear left onto Green Ridge Road (Road 11), drive 3.7 miles, and turn left on gravel Road 1110. The ample trailhead parking area is ahead in 5.3 miles.

The route starts northward around the butte, ascending steadily through a forest of ponderosa pines, some quite large. Small signs identify manzanita, chinkapin, snowbrush, and other understory plants at trailside. At 0.6 mile the forest's character changes suddenly, and becomes cooler, as you enter a grove dominated by grand fir. Round a switchback at 0.8 mile, and soon the trail emerges from the trees, granting views of Mount Washington and the Three Sisters. Look for scarlet gilia, balsam root, and

1924 lookout atop Black Butte

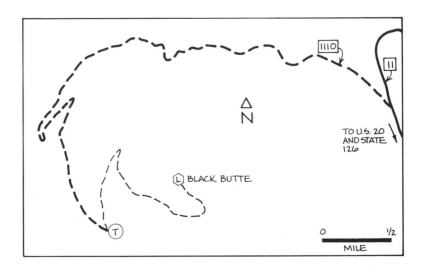

other wildflowers on the open slopes here in midsummer.

The view just gets better and better—of nearby mountains as well as of the manicured fairways of the resort below. Just before climbing onto the summit, the trail enters a grove of subalpine fir, then passes through an old burn, evidence of the 1981 Black Butte fire. Look east to see Smith Rock jutting from the high-desert floor.

Once on top, walk another minute to reach the base of the 85-foot lookout tower, built in 1934. There's plenty to see without climbing the tower, though it's hard to convince children of that (even with a sign that warns hikers away). Try redirecting children across the summit toward the 18-foot cupola lookout tower, built in 1924. A sign describes the development of fire lookout facilities on Black Butte, starting with an open platform constructed between two fir trees in 1910 and ending with the 1979 log cabin tucked just over the ridge near the cupola (occupied in summer, but not open to the public).

McKenzie River

State 126 and 242

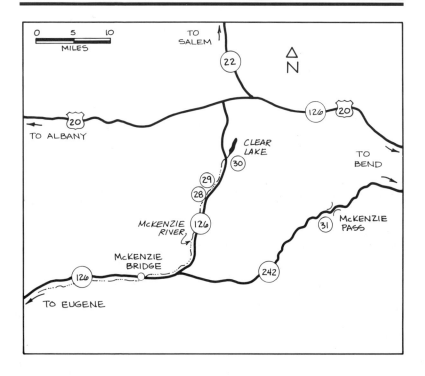

28. Tamolitch Pool

Type: Dayhike
Difficulty: Moderate
Distance: 4.6 miles round-trip
Hikable: Most of the year
Use: Light
High point: 2400 feet
Elevation gain: 200 feet
Maps: USGS Tamolitch Falls;
USFS McKenzie River
Trail brochure

The McKenzie River Trail offers a lot of opportunities for hikes, especially one-way treks with a shuttle car. It runs 26.5 miles from McKenzie Bridge north to Fish Lake, with about 10 access-road points along the way—and a corresponding number of sections to choose from for dayhikes.

The 2.3-mile hike from Trailbridge Reservoir to Tamolitch Pool is one good choice for a dayhike. It's uncrowded and low enough in elevation to be accessible much of the year, and it follows close to the river most of the way. The walk to the pool is fairly uneventful, but any child old enough to make the hike will appreciate the geological mystery at the hike's end: where does the water come from? It flows out of Tamolitch

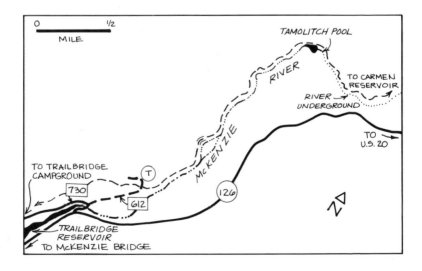

Counting tree rings along McKenzie River Trail

Pool—a deep, round, turquoise pond. Above the pond, however, the river disappears into porous lava rock underground as far upstream as Carmen Reservoir. (Some flow would probably be seen on the surface if much of the river weren't also diverted from Carmen to Smith Reservoir, reentering the McKenzie below Tamolitch.)

To reach the upper trailhead from McKenzie Bridge, take State 126 north about 15 miles and turn west onto Road 730 at the sign to Trailbridge Reservoir. After crossing the river, bear right up gravel Road 612 and drive 0.5 mile to a bend in the road, where you'll see the trailhead sign and enough parking for a few cars.

The trail is fairly level for the first 1.5 miles or so. The McKenzie River is placid and in sight much of the way. Cross a footbridge over a side creek after about 1 mile. About halfway to Tamolitch Pool the river picks up steam, tumbling and churning, as the trail gets a little steeper.

You'll know you're getting close to Tamolitch Pool when a lot of old lava rock appears on either side of the trail, even underfoot. The trail stays above the river, granting occasional views down to the rushing water. Then, suddenly, the rushing stops, and you'll be looking down into clear Tamolitch Pool from atop a rock cliff. A sign calls it Tamolitch Falls, and it's easy to imagine the dramatic waterfall that would tumble down the sheer cliff at the far end of the pool if flows were high enough.

Instead, the water seeps in invisibly. Explore the area a little, looking for tree molds left years ago when flowing lava surrounded standing trees.

With a shuttle car, Tamolitch Pool could serve as a stop on a one-way, downhill hike 5.2 miles from Carmen Reservoir to Trailbridge Reservoir.

29. Sahalie Falls–Koosah Falls Loop

Type:	Dayhike
Difficulty:	Moderate
Distance:	4 miles, loop
Hikable:	April through November
Use:	Heavy
High point:	3000 feet
Elevation gain:	400 feet
Maps:	USGS Clear Lake;
	USFS McKenzie River
	Trail brochure

Sahalie Falls and Koosah Falls are popular stopping points along the McKenzie River Highway. A link trail completed in 1991 enables hikers to make a 4-mile loop that takes in both falls. The forest is lush,

Ponderosa pine bough along McKenzie River

with tall trees, and the terrain is gentle. Kids will enjoy getting to see the two dramatic falls twice, plus crossing the McKenzie River on a high, narrow, log footbridge.

The hike can be started at several points; the simplest is the Sahalie Falls viewpoint, which has plenty of parking. From McKenzie Bridge, take State 126 north about 22 miles to the turnout at Sahalie Falls, on the west side of the road.

To hike counterclockwise, walk upriver, pausing to admire the falls from developed viewpoints along the way. Continue along the path 0.5 mile to its junction with the McKenzie River Trail. A right turn leads toward State 126 and Clear Lake; instead, turn left to cross a narrow footbridge over the rushing river.

The trail rolls downstream through old-growth trees and past a small outcrop of lava, leading back past Sahalie Falls, the foam at its base turning turquoise in sunlight. Continue down the trail, passing Koosah Falls about 0.7 mile past Sahalie. At about 2.5 miles, bear left at a trail

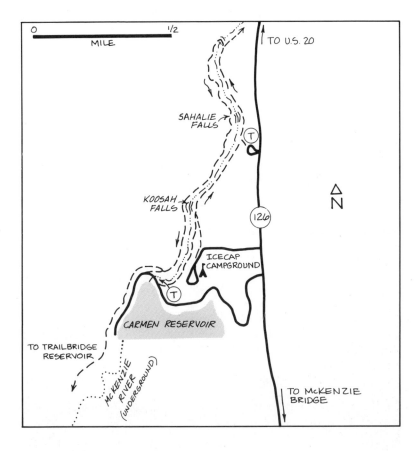

junction, leaving the McKenzie River Trail on a short spur leading to Carmen Reservoir.

The trail ends at the road around the reservoir. Follow the road to the left, across the McKenzie, then immediately look for a trail heading up the other side of the river. The trail up the east bank follows the river more closely. About 0.2 mile from the reservoir, pass a spur trail to Ice Cap Campground, then in another 0.2 mile arrive at a viewpoint over-looking Koosah Falls. Look for the springs gushing out of rocks at the base of the falls. The trail continues as a path and occasional stairs until it merges with the viewpoint trails at Sahalie Falls.

30. Clear Lake

Type:	Dayhike
Difficulty:	Moderate
Distance:	5 miles, loop
Hikable:	April through October
Use:	Heavy
High point:	3040 feet
Elevation gain:	Negligible
Maps:	USGS Clear Lake;
	Willamette National Forest

This has to be one of the best family hikes in this part of Oregon. Clear Lake is an exquisitely pure lake high in the mountains but just off State 126. The virtually level trail that encircles the lake passes through magnificent old-growth forest, winds along the sunny lakeshore, fords the McKenzie River on a log footbridge, and crosses over an extensive lava flow; it's interesting every step of the way. On the lake's west side, the hike follows a portion of the McKenzie River Trail (see Hikes 28 and 29, Tamolitch Pool and Sahalie Falls–Koosah Falls Loop). Along the lakeshore the route passes a campground and a picnic area as well as a small, rustic resort that rents rowboats by the hour. No motorboats are allowed on Clear Lake, thus preserving its purity and tranquility for hikers and boaters alike. Wear sturdy-soled boots; ankle-twisting lava rocks are sharp through thin soles.

 From McKenzie Bridge, drive north on State 126 about 23 miles and turn right at the sign to Coldwater Cove Campground. Follow the road around to the boat ramp at the end of the campground and park in the parking area. The hike could also be started at the resort and picnic area

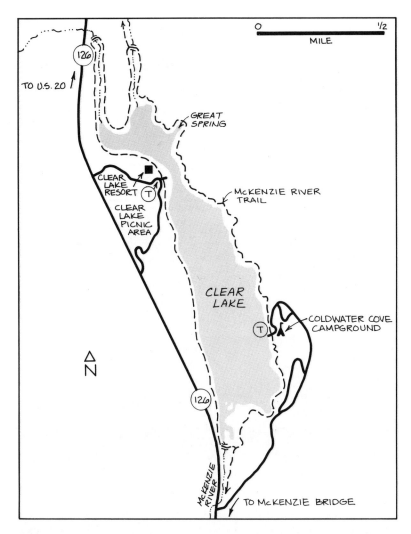

on the other side of the lake, but a counterclockwise hike from Coldwater Cove gets kids onto the intriguing lava flow quickly and gets the hottest part of the hike over with while they're fresh.

Head north on the McKenzie River Trail through big trees, passing lots of anglers' spur trails to the lake. Soon the dirt-surface trail turns to asphalt when it reaches the lava flow. The vine maple here turns color sooner than in the forest, due to the stress of living with little water and among hot rocks. Continue across the lava for about 0.4 mile.

Enter the forest, then reemerge onto another 0.4-mile-wide lava flow. Reenter the woods and shortly pass a clear, blue-green cove—the site

Footbridge across McKenzie River at Clear Lake

 of Great Springs, one of the largest of several springs that feed Clear Lake. Past the cove, look for evidence of ants and woodpeckers in huge, trailside Douglas firs.

At 1.8 miles cross a streambed on a footbridge. At the end of the bridge, at a trail junction, the McKenzie River Trail heads to the right; bear left instead, heading around the north end of the lake. At a trailside bench there's a good view south to the Three Sisters. Following an inlet creek, the trail approaches the highway, then crosses the creek and heads back towards the lake. Clear Lake Resort is at about 3 miles; continue a short distance past the resort cabins and store and up the paved road. Leave the road near the picnic area's restrooms, where the

trail resumes. Cross a small, musical creek, then cross the lake's outlet—
the McKenzie River—on a massive footbridge at 4.1 miles. In 0.1 mile
the McKenzie River Trail is encountered again; follow it to the left 0.8
mile more, along the lakeshore and across a lava flow, to find yourself
back at the parking area.

31. Proxy Falls

Type:	Dayhike
Difficulty:	Easy
Distance:	1.3 miles round-trip
Hikable:	June through October
Use:	Heavy
High point:	3200 feet
Elevation gain:	Negligible
Maps:	USGS Linton Lake;
	Willamette National Forest

For a short hike to a couple of spectacular waterfalls, this trail is a
good choice. The highway leading to the trailhead closes in winter; shortly
after it opens, the rhododendrons start blooming along the trail. A hike

Fork in rock-lined Proxy Falls Trail

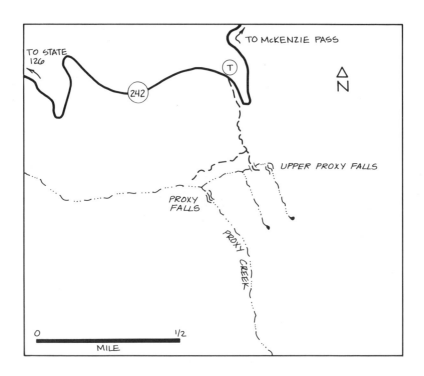

to Proxy Falls is a great way to break up a trip between Eugene and Sisters.

 From the junction of state highways 126 and 242, take State 242 (the old McKenzie scenic route) east 9 miles and park along the road by a small hiker sign. (The sign is hard to spot; the trailhead is also 1.6 miles west of Alder Springs Campground.)

From the trailhead, climb up a bit, then follow an old lava flow brimming with vine maple. Past the lava, walk through a Douglas fir forest with big rhododendrons and lots of beargrass. Cross a little wooden bridge at 0.3 mile, then immediately reach a junction. Bear left; the base of Upper Proxy Falls is reached in 0.1 mile. Here water from springs high above fall more than 100 feet over a stair-step cliff thick with velvety moss. The placid pool at the base is inviting for toe-dipping or exploring. Receptive children and adults will enjoy the parklike atmosphere of the forest here.

Back at the junction, follow the sign 0.25 mile to the Proxy Falls viewpoint. Across an expanse of forest Proxy Creek can be seen sliding 200 feet down a curved cliff face, as if outlining a vase. Return as you came, bearing left at the trail junction.

Central Oregon

U.S. 97 and Cascade Lakes Highway

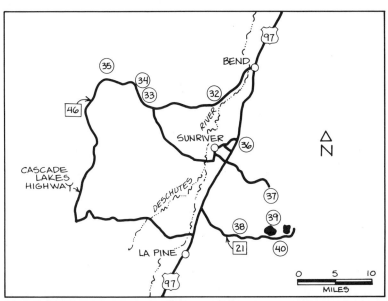

Volcanic rock, Lava Cast Forest

32. Deschutes River Trail: Lava Island

Type: Dayhike
Difficulty: Easy
Distance: 1.25 miles one way
Hikable: Most of the year
Use: Heavy
High point: 4100 feet
Elevation gain: 120 feet
Elevation loss: 320 feet
Maps: USGS Benham Falls;
Deschutes National Forest

Someday hikers will be able to follow the Deschutes River from its headwaters in the Cascade Lakes north through Bend and nearly to the northern border of Deschutes County. Several sections of the Deschutes River Trail have been completed; this one, closer to town (and lower in elevation) than many Bend-area hikes, leads past an island of lava to a rock shelter believed to have been used by various indigenous peoples over the past 7000 years. Hike it as a round-trip hike or one way with a shuttle car. After hiking this section you may want to try others; south of Lava Island, for instance, the trail continues 3.25 miles to Dillon Falls.

Rock shelter along Deschutes River Trail

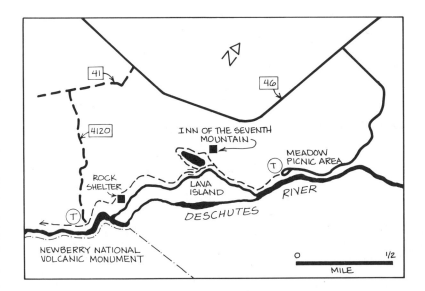

NEWBERRY NATIONAL
VOLCANIC MONUMENT

From Bend, follow signs toward Mount Bachelor and Century Drive (which becomes Cascade Lakes Highway and Road 46). About 5 miles from Bend, turn left at the sign to Meadow Picnic Area. (If you pass Inn of the Seventh Mountain resort, you've gone about a mile too far.) Continue 1.5 miles to the trailhead parking area at road's end.

The trail follows the hillside between the Deschutes River and rimrock. In a couple of minutes an island of lava splits the river; follow the island all the way to the end of this hike. Notice the few hardy ponderosa pines growing out of the lava.

About 0.5 mile from the Meadow Picnic Area trailhead there's a junction at the end of a small lake. A right turn leads on a detour around the lake (or up to Inn of the Seventh Mountain). Continuing straight, pass the lake's marshy outlet, home to a variety of moisture-loving plants and animals, including, in summer, hummingbirds, kingfishers, and rather bloodthirsty mosquitoes. Pass another junction, walk along a moist berm, cross a footbridge, and then climb a little higher on the hillside, away from the lake.

A few minutes from the trail's end at Lava Island day-use area, the trail passes the rock shelter. Archeologists believe it was used as a hunters' camp, because of the ancient tools and supplies found stored here. Children won't need much encouragement to crawl inside; when they do, suggest they think about what life might have been like for the ancient people who camped here. How different was their view out the cave?

A few minutes beyond the shelter there's a parking area with restrooms adjacent to the southern end of Lava Island. To drive here with a shuttle car, or to start the hike here, continue east on Cascade Lakes Highway

from the road to Meadow Picnic Area. About 0.2 mile past Inn of the
Seventh Mountain, turn left onto Forest Road 41. Drive 0.3 mile, turn
left onto Road 4120, go 0.8 mile, and turn left at the sign to Lava Island
Rock Shelter.

33. Tumalo Mountain

Type:	Dayhike
Difficulty:	Moderate to difficult
Distance:	4 miles round-trip
Hikable:	July through October
Use:	Light
High point:	7775 feet
Elevation gain:	1415 feet
Maps:	USGS Broken Top and
	Bachelor Butte;
	Deschutes National Forest

If a child were to ask, "What's it like to climb a mountain?" what
would you say? Perhaps something like, "Well, it's usually a long hike, and

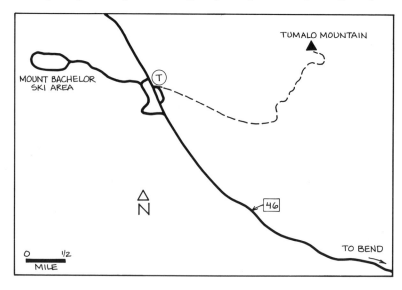

Three Sisters and Broken Top from Tumalo Mountain summit

it's really steep at the end. But when you get to the top you feel like you're at the top of the world, and you feel a really good kind of tired."

Tumalo Mountain can give children a taste of mountain climbing in a relatively short outing. The hike begins as a gradual but steady ascent through a forest, then breaks into the open and steepens radically for the final ascent. At the top, you're clearly not on top of the world (Mount Bachelor is close enough that you'll feel you could hit it with a well-aimed rock, but it's 1290 feet higher), but the panorama is grand, with views of Broken Top's crater, the Three Sisters, Sparks Lake, the verdant Tumalo Creek drainage, Bend, and even Smith Rock in the distance. It can be chilly and windy at the top; be sure to carry an extra shirt or windbreaker for lingering on the summit.

From Bend, follow Century Drive (which becomes Cascade Lakes Highway and Road 46) about 25 miles to the Mount Bachelor ski area. Just past the first Mount Bachelor turn-off (3 miles west of the Sunriver cut-off road), turn right at the sign to the Tumalo Mountain trailhead parking area. In winter, this is a large snow-park area.

The trail winds uphill, alternating between forest and meadow; peek through the trees to see the ski runs on Mount Bachelor. Point out to children how contorted some of the trees are, a result of being under snow more than half the year.

For the final 0.5 mile, the forest falls away and you walk straight up the steep trail to the summit. This is a good place to teach children the "wedding march" style of hiking, emulating climbers, as an alternative to the hike-rest-hike-rest style that kids can fall into. When they do rest, kids who ski in winter will get a kick out of seeing Mount Bachelor's snow-free runs so clearly etched among the trees. On the return hike, they may wish they had ski poles to help them schuss down the steep summit trail.

34. Todd Lake

Type:	Dayhike
Difficulty:	Easy
Distance:	2.4 miles, loop
Hikable:	July through October
Use:	Heavy
High point:	6150 feet
Elevation gain:	Negligible
Maps:	USGS Broken Top; Deschutes National Forest

The southern end of picturesque, forty-five-acre Todd Lake is perhaps 0.2 mile from the trailhead parking area, making it a popular spot for camping on late-summer weekends. That accessibility also makes it appealing for an easy, level hike. Count on mosquitoes early in the season;

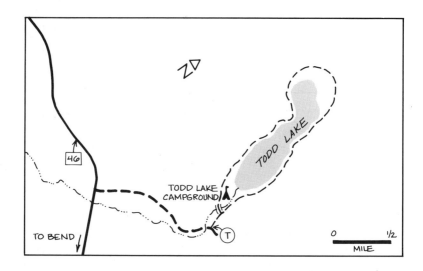

Todd Lake

all season, wear boots (or expect soggy sneakers) for walking around the lake's marshy far end.

From Bend, follow Century Drive (which becomes Cascade Lakes Highway and Road 46) about 25 miles toward the Mount Bachelor ski area. About 1.5 miles past Mount Bachelor, turn right at the sign to Todd Lake and drive 0.5 mile to the parking area above the meadow. Begin hiking up the gated road marked with a campground sign.

A couple of minutes up the road, it splits; you can go in either direction to circle Todd Lake. Going clockwise, cross the lake's outlet to reach a small campground on the lakeshore; Broken Top can be seen rising beyond the water. Walk to the lake edge and pick up the trail, which follows the shore closely.

Wildflowers border the trail here and there; occasionally you'll step over wet spots where springs are seeping into the lake. Approaching the lake's far end, cross rivulets that zigzag across a widening meadow. The trail per se disappears at the far end, where the terrain gets very soggy; pick a route to stay as dry as possible.

Pick up the trail where the marsh gives way to drier ground. The trail then reenters the forest, following close to the lake's east shore for the walk back to the junction.

35. Moraine Lake

Type:	Dayhike (backpacking not recommended)
Difficulty:	Moderate to difficult
Distance:	4.5 miles round-trip
Hikable:	July through October
Use:	Heavy
High point:	6650 feet
Elevation gain:	1350 feet
Maps:	USGS South Sister; Deschutes National Forest

What makes this hike so rewarding is the opportunity to see a pristine alpine lake in an awesome glacial cirque after just 2.25 miles of hiking. Located within Three Sisters Wilderness, Moraine Lake is popular with weekend backpackers; for the lake's sake, camp elsewhere and dayhike to the lake. If overnighting here, resist the temptation to camp right on the lakeshore, where it's impossible to avoid damaging the fragile vegetation and tainting the lake.

What makes the hike rather difficult is the relentless, and often steep, initial 1.5 miles without so much as a view to enjoy or a creek to cross. Take children who can handle a little delayed gratification.

 From Bend, follow Century Drive (which becomes Cascade Lakes Highway and Road 46) about 25 miles toward the Mount Bachelor ski area. About 6 miles past Mount Bachelor, turn left at the sign to Devil's Lake and Wickiup Plains. At the far end of the parking area, look for the sign to South Sister Climbers Trail.

Follow the trail across a creek and across the highway, where the trail starts up, first ascending a hillside and then climbing up a forested

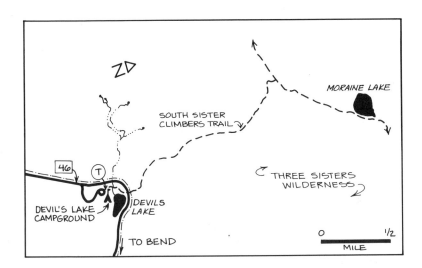

ravine. The grade varies between moderate and steep for 1.5 miles, until you emerge from the trees onto an open ridge and see South Sister and Broken Top ahead and to the right. There's a trail junction here; climbers continue straight, but you'll turn right toward Moraine Lake.

The trail crosses a sandy moonscape, dropping down into a basin and up a short rise before dropping again to the lake, a gorgeous alpine gem seemingly cupped in the mountain's palm. After a rest, children may find themselves compelled to explore the open alpine landscape around the lake or play hide-and-seek in the tree islands above it.

Broken Top, seen from trail to Moraine Lake

36. Lava River Cave

Type: Dayhike
Difficulty: Easy
Distance: 2 miles round-trip
Hikable: Mid-May through mid-September
Use: Heavy
High point: 4500 feet
Elevation gain: 200 feet
Map: USFS Lava River Cave brochure

Hiking in a cave? When the cave is a mile-long uncollapsed lava tube, you bet! The cave is part of Newberry Crater National Monument, so designated in 1990. The Forest Service keeps the cave open to visitors during the summer, charging a small admission fee and another fifty cents or so for lantern rental. Take a flashlight for back-up light, but rent a lantern as well; you can see much more than with a flashlight, and responsible children can take turns holding the light. Be sure to wear warm clothes as well; regardless of the temperature outside, the cave is always about 40° F.

Children will be awed by the whole experience: the darkness broken by the lanterns' light and the long shadows they cast, the eerie sounds of hissing lanterns and echoing voices, and just the knowledge that they're under the earth, out of touch with familiar landmarks. Some may be a little frightened and will need reassurance. Adventurous types may need

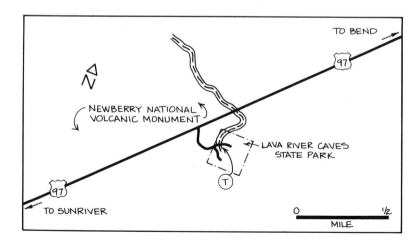

Emerging from Lava River Cave

reminders not to wander too far from the light; it's easy to twist an ankle wandering alone in the dark. But rest assured there are no side chambers to wander into mistakenly.

From Bend, take U.S. 97 south about 12 miles and turn east at the sign to Lava River Cave. Pick up a free trail brochure at the entrance booth for interpretation along the way or for reading after the hike.

You enter the lava tube at a point where, ages ago, the roof collapsed. Look back to see that the tube actually continues in the other direction (but is currently blocked off). Stairs lead down into the cave; once on the cave floor, begin a slow descent on a rock and sand surface with a few stairs here and there. About 0.25 mile from the entrance, the lava tube crosses under the highway (don't bother listening for cars; they're a good 80 feet above you). Then at about 0.6 mile look for the Sand

Garden, where dripping water has created a fantastical landscape in a field of sand that has slowly entered the cave over centuries. The hike ends after 1 mile, where sand blocks further progress in the tube.

Like other lava tubes, Lava River Cave was formed when a flow of hot lava from Newberry Volcano began to cool and crusted over. The lava inside the flow drained out, leaving it an empty tube. The "river" refers to the river of lava; geologists believe no river of water ever flowed in the cave.

37. Lava Cast Forest

Type: Dayhike
Difficulty: Easy
Distance: 0.9 mile, loop
Hikable: June through October
Use: Heavy
High point: 5820 feet
Elevation gain: Negligible
Maps: Deschutes National Forest;
USFS Lava Cast Forest:
Walk through Time brochure

This isn't so much a hike as a paved nature walk, but the terrain it covers is so unusual it's worth seeking out. The path winds through a moonscape of lava, passing tree molds formed when hot lava swirled

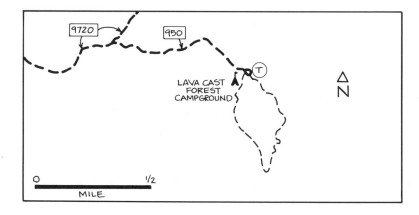

Climbing into lava-cast tree well

around the forest, burning the trees but leaving hardened lava molds where they had stood. This hike is just a short drive from Sunriver, though the last 9 miles of road are rather long and washboardy.

From Bend, drive south 13 miles on U.S. 97 and turn east onto Road 9720 (directly across the road from the turn-off to Sunriver). Follow the road (turns to gravel in 0.2 mile) 8.7 miles and turn right on Road 950 at the sign to Lava Cast Forest; continue 0.5 mile to the trailhead at road's end.

Pick up an interpretive pamphlet, if any, at the trailhead; descriptions correspond to numbered posts along the way. The path loops through the open lava field, treeless but for a few ponderosa pines growing out of cracks in the lava. Kids will have a great time peeking around, and even climbing into, the many lava tree molds along the route. With little shade, it's a hot spot in midsummer; come early or late on a summer day, when the low sun gives color to the dark rock.

38. Peter Skene Ogden Trail

Type: Dayhike
Difficulty: Easy to difficult
Distance: 2.75 miles one way, lower section; 5.75 miles one way, upper section
Hikable: June through October
Use: Light
High point: 4720 feet, lower section; 6330 feet, upper section
Elevation gain: 420 feet, lower section; 1610 feet, upper section
Maps: USGS Finley Butte and Paulina Peak; Deschutes National Forest

The 8.5-mile trail following Paulina Creek from Paulina Lake, at Newberry Crater, down the volcano's pine-forested slope offers waterfalls, wading, and pleasant creekside hiking. The trip can be hot and dusty midday in midsummer; go early or late in the day. Better yet, try it in late spring, when the waterfalls are gushing, or autumn, when aspen leaves flutter gold against the red ponderosa pines.

Road access at McKay Crossing splits the trail into two sections. With a shuttle car you can hike the entire trail, or just hike the upper or lower section one way. Older kids might enjoy the challenge of hiking the entire trail top-to-bottom (a moderate to difficult hike); most youngsters will find that one section is enough. With its gentle grade and proximity to U.S. 97, the lower section is the best choice for a moderately easy round-trip hike; hence, the trail is described here bottom-to-top. Families overnighting alongside one of the two lakes in the crater might enjoy the short hike down the trail to Paulina Creek Falls (1 mile round-trip).

About 20 miles south of Bend on U.S. 97, turn east on Forest Road 21 at the sign to Newberry Volcano. Go 2.8 miles and turn left at the

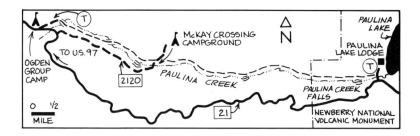

sign for Ogden Group Camp, then follow signs 0.3 mile to the trailhead. To reach McKay Crossing by car, continue up Road 21 another 0.5 mile, turn left at the sign to McKay Crossing Campground, and follow the road 2.3 miles to the campground; the trail starts on a rise just across the creek.

From the lower trailhead, walk up some steps, then walk about 50 yards to a sturdy pole footbridge crossing Paulina Creek. The trail heads up the creek's south bank, following it closely most of the way to another bridge at 0.9 mile. This is a good spot to picnic or dip toes; the creek is fairly shallow and safe.

From the bridge, the trail steepens a bit, but not much. It veers away from the creek much of the way to McKay Crossing—always in earshot, but not always in view—passing through a forest of lodgepole and ponderosa pines. About 0.25 mile short of McKay Crossing, the creek cascades into a rocky gorge; you have to walk off the trail a few steps for a good view, but take care in doing so. This is a good turnaround if you're hiking back the way you came—the campground just ahead is uninteresting, but the creek does flatten out there, for those in need of a refreshing wade. (There's also an outhouse, but no drinking water.) The final 0.25 mile of this lower trail section swings away from the creek, passing the campground, and leads to the McKay Crossing.

Hiking the upper trail section from McKay Crossing, the trail is a bit steeper. It follows the creek fairly closely, in view of several minifalls along the way. About 0.5 mile before the trail's end at Paulina Lake, the creek drops 100 feet to form Paulina Creek Falls.

The trail emerges next to the bridge on the short access road from Road 21 to Paulina Lake Lodge. Cars can be left in a wide parking area south of the boat dock or in a picnic area just up Road 21.

39. Paulina Lake Shoreline

Type: Dayhike
Difficulty: Moderate to difficult
Distance: 7.5 miles, loop
Hikable: June through October
Use: Heavy
High point: 6555 feet
Elevation gain: 195 feet
Maps: USGS Paulina Peak and
East Lake; Deschutes
National Forest

Why walk around a lake that's accessible by car? In the case of Paulina Lake, three reasons come to mind: to get to some otherwise inaccessible parts of the shoreline, to see the lake and surrounding country from a different perspective, and, perhaps most of all, to get the sense of accomplishment that accompanies such a trek. Though motorboats slowly trolling on the lake keep you from feeling "away from it all," the lake attracts more anglers than hikers and you're likely to be alone on much of the trail. This hike is recommended for older children who enjoy a challenge. For a shorter hike (4 miles one way), leave a shuttle car at Little Crater Campground.

About 20 miles south of Bend on U.S. 97, turn east on Forest Road 21 at the sign to Newberry Volcano. Follow it 13 miles to the crater rim and turn left toward Paulina Lake Lodge, parking in the lot south of the boat ramp.

To walk clockwise, head toward the lodge along the shore to a trail sign and the beginning of a footpath. The trail reaches a nice gravel beach and campsite (with outhouse) and view of Paulina Peak at about 1.25 miles. At 2 miles, the trail leads away from the lake and up the hill

(the only significant ascent on the trail) to avoid a steep, red rockslide along the lake.

Back down near lake level, notice the way the trail sparkles with tiny chips of obsidian; they're from an obsidian flow a few minutes ahead on the trail. The shoreline grows rockier here, more dramatic, on the approach to Little Crater Campground, at 4 miles.

Walk through the campground on the road for about 0.5 mile until the trail resumes along the now sandy lakeshore. Pass in front of some privately owned summer homes and into a wide, grassy marsh teeming with butterflies and dragonflies. The trail reenters forest, crossing creeks

Paulina Lake

on little footbridges, to emerge again at Paulina Lake Campground. Follow signs and trail marker posts past the boat ramp, through the willows, and up to the road bridge crossing Paulina Creek, the lake's outlet, and back to the parking lot.

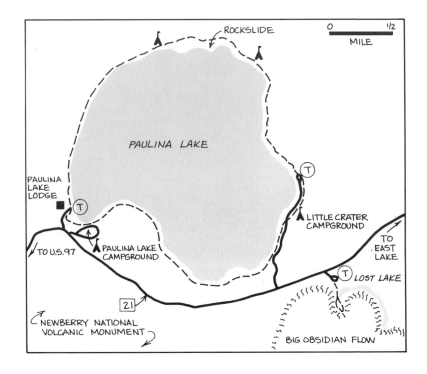

40. Obsidian Flow

Type:	Dayhike
Difficulty:	Easy
Distance:	0.7 mile, loop
Hikable:	June through October
Use:	Heavy
High point:	6600 feet
Elevation gain:	100 feet
Maps:	USGS East Lake;
	Deschutes National Forest

Though this trail is too short to qualify as a real hike—it's really a short interpretive trail—make a point of walking it on a visit to Newberry Crater. Even in the volcanic Oregon Cascades, it's unlikely you'll see another mountain of black, glasslike obsidian. It's fascinating, and it offers

Footbridge across chasm in Obsidian Flow

adults an opportunity to explain how glass is made from sand—a process similar to the way this obsidian was made deep inside the now-dormant volcano. A paved trail completed in 1990 leads safely up onto the flow. Keep the kids on the trail; off-trail, the obsidian is literally as slick and sharp as glass.

About 20 miles south of Bend on U.S. 97, turn east on Forest Road 21 at the sign to Newberry Volcano. Follow it 13 miles to the crater rim, then continue on the main road 2.3 miles to the sign for "Obsidian Flow."

The path threads through lodgepole pines to a staircase that leads up and onto the obsidian flow; look over your left shoulder to see aptly named Lost Lake. Cross a chasm on a sturdy footbridge, then turn right or left to make the loop. Short spur trails lead to benches and viewpoints. From the highest point there's a magnificent view not only of the obsidian flow surrounding you but of Paulina Peak, Paulina Lake, and South, Middle, and the tip of North Sister.

The obsidian flow was formed during an eruption of the caldera between Paulina and East lakes less than 1900 years ago. The rock under the caldera was rich in silica, the main ingredient in glass; when it melted from the heat of the earth, and later cooled, obsidian was formed. Notice the few scraggy pines that have managed to grow seemingly out of bare rock—but really in niches where water and a little soil have accumulated over the centuries.

Willamette Pass

State 58

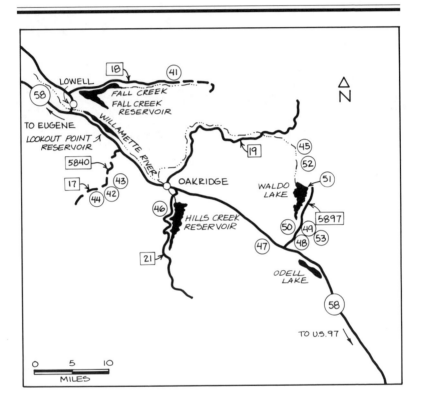

41. Fall Creek Trail

Type: Dayhike
Difficulty: Easy to moderate
Distance: 1.7 to 4.1 miles, per section,
one way
Hikable: Most of the year
Use: Heavy
High point: 1600 feet
Elevation gain: Negligible to 240 feet
Maps: USGS Saddleblanket Mountain
and Sinker Mountain;
USFS Fall Creek National
Recreation Trail brochure

What makes Fall Creek Trail so appealing isn't its drama—it's a pretty low-key path along a low-elevation mountain creek. Rather, what makes it so popular with families is big trees, a gorgeous narrow canyon and sparkling, ice-cold stream, a sprinkling of footbridges, lots of options for one-way and round-trip hikes, and proximity to Eugene. So, for families living in or near Eugene and looking for a short, nearby forest hike by a cool creek in midsummer, or a nearby, snow-free hike in November, consider Fall Creek. It may become a habit.

The road meets the 14-mile-long trail at five points, naturally dividing the trail into four chunks that each can be walked one way with a shuttle car, or combined with another section for a longer hike. Following are trail descriptions for the first three sections, each described as a downstream (east to west) hike. Also consider a stroll along either of two nature loop trails: Clark Creek and Johnny Creek.

To reach Fall Creek from Eugene, take I-5 south to State 58 and follow it 13 miles, exiting at the town of Lowell. From Lowell, follow signs 3 miles north to the Unity covered bridge and turn right onto Fall Creek

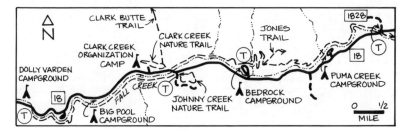

Road. Follow it 10 miles (it becomes Road 18) to the start of the trail, across the road from Dolly Varden Campground.

Johnny Creek to Dolly Varden Campground, 3.5 miles. This is a fun section; but as the first section, it gets the most use, and the road is often in sight, albeit across the creek. The upper trailhead is near

Footbridge across Bedrock Creek

Johnny Creek Nature Trail, 3 miles up Road 18 from Dolly Varden, where the road crosses Fall Creek. The safest parking is at the start of the nature trail, just off Road 18 on the right; walk the short distance back to Road 18, then head west following the gravel road on the creek's south bank.

It's a little confusing in here, with various side trails leading every which way. The simplest route is to follow the gravel road about 0.3 mile to an informal campground and pick up the trail that bears right, down toward the creek.

At 0.5 mile the trail leads over a wonderful log bridge that crosses bedrock-lined Timber Creek. Back along Fall Creek the trail hugs the bank, about as close as you can get without wading. Follow the trail's ups and downs over three little footbridges. You'll know you're at about the 2-mile point when you see railing across the river indicating Big Pool Campground. The last 1.5 miles roll along next to the now-placid creek, with several more footbridge crossings before hitting the lower trailhead.

Bedrock Campground to Johnny Creek, 1.7 miles. The high point of this short stretch is a wonderful swimming hole at Slick Creek. The upper trailhead is at Bedrock Campground, on the north side of Road 18 4.4 miles east of Dolly Varden. Drive into the campground and follow the camping loop. At the far end of the loop, turn right into a large, signed trailhead parking area.

Follow the trail through the trees, bearing right at a junction at 0.25 mile (a left turn loops back to the campground). The level trail now follows just above the creek. Rather treacherous little skid trails lead down to the creek at various points; try to restrain the kids and wait until a substantial footbridge over Slick Creek is reached at about 0.6 mile; here there's easy access to good swimming and wading spots, a beach, and flat rocks for lazing around.

At about the halfway point the trail starts climbing briefly, then drops. Cross creeks on two more footbridges before meeting the road at the start of Clark Butte Trail and the end of this trail section.

Road 1828 to Bedrock Campground, 4.1 miles. This section is the most remote of the three and the least level, with an elevation gain of more than 200 feet. The upper trailhead is on the north side of Road 18 at the start of Road 1828, 7 miles east of Dolly Varden.

The trail here is narrow, but easy to follow and relatively level, and runs through a lovely forest of big trees alongside the exquisite creek. At 0.3 mile, cross a side creek on a log bridge. At about 0.8 mile, notice the fantastical rock formations on the stream; if kids are old enough, this is a nice swimming hole and sunning spot on a hot day.

At about 1.3 miles the trail starts veering away from the creek and into a grove of magnificent old-growth trees. Another 0.2 mile of hiking leads to a crest above the creek. The trail then drops slightly, crossing Jones Creek on a long log bridge. From there, the trail leads away from the creek again and begins a serious climb. The trail isn't steep, but the

Swordfern fiddleheads

hillside is, and the trail gets a little rockier. At about 2.8 miles, after a couple of switchbacks, the trail's crest is reached at a little peeled-log bench with a view of a clearcut and, below it, a farm.

As the trail descends (then ascends a bit, then drops again) over the next 0.5 mile, notice how the vegetation changes to reflect a drier microclimate, with oaks and madrones in addition to cedars and Douglas firs. At 3.3 miles, bear left at the junction with Jones Trail. Now the trail starts its real descent, switchbacking into a grove of rhododendrons; listen as the sound of Fall Creek grows louder. At the junction, a sign for Fall Creek Trail points to the right; follow it 0.25 mile and across pretty Bedrock Creek (pausing to hunt for crawdads) to the trailhead at Bedrock Campground.

42. Spirit Falls

Type: Dayhike
Difficulty: Easy
Distance: 0.7 mile round-trip
Hikable: Most of the year
Use: Light
High point: 2000 feet
Elevation gain: 200 feet
Maps: USGS Rose Hill;
Umpqua National Forest

Just the names of this and the next waterfall hike are alluring enough, and they fulfill their promise of magic to hikers, especially those visiting in spring, when stream flows are high, or in summer, when cooling mists from the falls are most welcome. Combine a hike to Spirit Falls with a hike to Moon Falls, down the road, and possibly with Swordfern Trail, also in the neighborhood, for a full day's outings in the Layng Creek watershed. These three trails are also accessible from Cottage Grove; from Eugene, the following road directions (off State 58) get you to the falls most quickly.

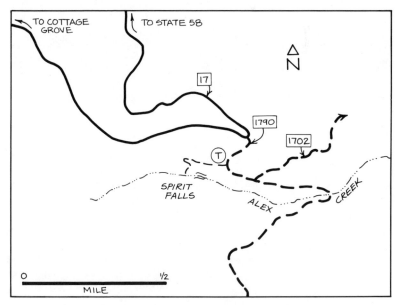

Spirit Falls

 From I-5 in Eugene, take State 58 southeast and turn south on Patterson Mountain Road (Road 5840), past milepost 25. Follow this gravel road 9.7 miles up and over Patterson Saddle (where it becomes Road 17) and down to Road 1790; turn left. Immediately to the right is a wide spot—the trailhead for Spirit Falls.

The trail drops gently, levels somewhat, and then begins to drop rather steeply down a dirt path that's slippery when wet. It ends at the base of 60-foot Spirit Falls, which gushes over domed cliffs. There's a picnic table at a viewpoint overlooking the falls, and the pool at the base of the umbrellalike falls is small and inviting for wading (though swimming, per se, is prohibited in the Layng Creek watershed).

43. Moon Falls

Type: Dayhike
Difficulty: Easy
Distance: 1 mile round-trip
Hikable: Most of the year
Use: Light
High point: 3100 feet
Elevation gain: 100 feet
Maps: USGS Holland Point;
Umpqua National Forest

A hike to 125-foot Moon Falls is a gentle, easy outing for young children. Listen for the low booming of grouse on the hike in.

Follow the directions to Spirit Falls (Hike 42) to get to Road 1790.

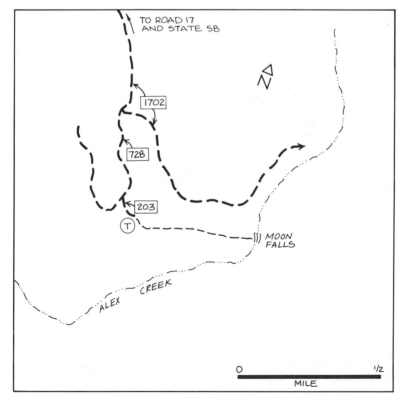

Sightseeing on Moon Falls Trail

Drive 0.2 mile past the Spirit Falls trailhead and bear left on Road 1702. Drive 2.8 miles and turn right on Road 1702-728. Go 0.3 mile and bear left on Road 1702-203 and continue 0.1 mile to the trailhead, where further progress by vehicles is blocked.

Begin the hike by walking along the overgrown spur road. At about 0.3 mile the route turns into a narrow forest footpath as it approaches Moon Falls. The trail ends at the base of the falls, which streams down a broad cliff in rivulets that run together before plunging into the pool below. Plan to linger a while at the falls, exploring the pool and Alex Creek and perhaps having lunch at the picnic table there (though wind-fallen trees have made it difficult to reach the table).

44. Swordfern Trail

Type:	Dayhike
Difficulty:	Easy
Distance:	1.5 miles, loop
Hikable:	Most of the year
Use:	Light
High point:	1500 feet
Elevation gain:	250 feet
Maps:	USGS Rose Hill; Umpqua National Forest

Swordfern Trail is a good choice for a short, get-away-from-the-crowds hike in the woods. It's little used, and it's in deep forest. Adults will enjoy its serenity; kids will enjoy the creek and the footbridges crossing its tributaries, the big trees and big stumps left by early loggers, the old log shelter near the trailhead, and all the other details adults often miss. In May the trail is lined with blooming wild iris and trillium.

Follow directions to Spirit Falls (Hike 42) but continue on Road 17 another 7 miles past Road 1790, turning left into Rujada Campground. Coming from Cottage Grove, follow signs toward Dorena Lake on Row River Road. About 19 miles from Cottage Grove, turn left onto Layng Creek Road, which becomes Forest Road 17. Go 2 miles and turn right into Rujada Campground.

From the signed trailhead parking area, the trail rolls alongside pretty Layng Creek through a lush forest. There are plenty of sword ferns; how many other kinds of ferns can the kids find? Footbridges cross several side creeks trickling into the main creek.

At about 0.5 mile the trail starts to climb, rising into the forest above the creek as it makes a wide turn to head back in the other direction. In here, check the big stumps for springboard cuts. Notice the small gullies created by log skidding nearly 100 years ago. At 0.7 mile the trail

Taking shelter near start of Swordfern Trail

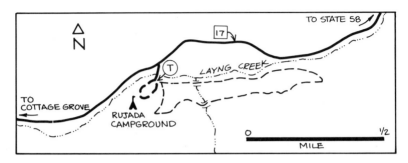

turns into an abandoned logging road, long reclaimed by grasses and ferns. After about 0.25 mile, it returns to a narrow forest footpath and drops back down the hill into the campground.

45. Erma Bell Lakes

Type:	Dayhike (backpacking not recommended)
Difficulty:	Moderate
Distance:	5.5 miles round-trip
Hikable:	July through October
Use:	Heavy
High point:	4700 feet
Elevation gain:	250 feet
Maps:	USGS Waldo Mountain; Willamette National Forest

Three mountain lakes are perfectly spaced along a moderately graded trail, as if custom-ordered by a hiking family. The first lake is a pleasant 1.75 miles in, then 0.5 mile to the next, and 0.5 mile to the one after that. Middle Erma Bell is a beauty, and it's the best place to pause and picnic with children; the shoreline is gentle, neither rocky like the lower sister nor mucky like the upper. It's a popular trail; consider hiking it in late autumn, when the huckleberry and vine maple are ablaze and fellow hikers are few.

 From the Oakridge Ranger Station (32 miles southeast of I-5 on State 58), turn north at the sign to Westfir. Drive 0.4 mile, turn left, and continue 32.4 miles up North Fork Road (Road 19). At Box Canyon, turn right on gravel Road 1957 and drive 3.7 miles to Skookum Creek Campground and the trailhead. On the way in or out, stop to let the kids explore the "old" cabin near the road in Box Canyon. It's really a replica of Landis Cabin, built here in 1918 as a Forest Service fire guard station. The original cabin was destroyed by vandals in 1969; its replica was built in 1972.

Cross Skookum Creek on a wide footbridge and immediately enter Three Sisters Wilderness. At 0.5 mile, bear right at the junction with Otter Lake Trail. Continue climbing gently; at about 1 mile, descend for 0.3 mile or so, cross a creek, climb again, and at 1.75 mile reach a fork; Lower Erma Bell lies about 80 yards down the spur trail to the left. Watch for water ouzels flitting about the scree-covered southern shoreline.

Back on the main trail, cross the lake's outlet and follow the trail along the lake's edge, climbing gently through an impressive rhododendron grove. Lower Erma Bell is still in sight when Middle Erma Bell comes into view. A spur trail leads down to it; the main trail continues past the lake, granting only glimmering glimpses of it through the forest.

Lower Erma Bell Lake

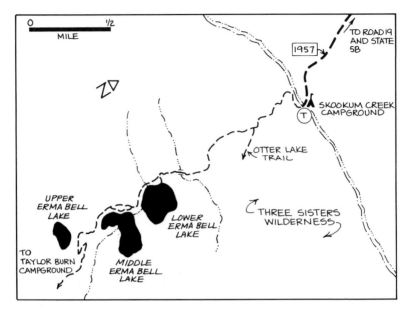

About a minute after the middle lake can no longer be seen, Upper Erma Bell comes into view—the smallest of the three lakes, not much more than a pond. The trail continues 1.75 miles to Taylor Burn Campground, a very rough 8-mile drive north of Waldo Lake.

46. Larison Cove

Type:	Dayhike or backpack
Difficulty:	Easy to moderate
Distance:	4 miles round-trip
Hikable:	Year-round
Use:	Heavy
High point:	1600 feet
Elevation gain:	Negligible
Maps:	USGS Oakridge;
	Willamette National Forest

Just outside of Oakridge, Hills Creek Reservoir stretches to the south, reaching its many arms into mountain creek valleys and creating isolated coves. One particularly long cove, Larison, has an easy, quietly scenic trail following its north bank. It's rated heavy use, but just barely. No motorized boats are allowed on this cove—in fact, picnic areas have been developed on the south shore specifically to encourage canoeing—adding to the peaceful charm of the trail. The entire trail is more than 6 miles long, but most families will stop at the footbridge at the 2-mile point, near the head of the cove. Picnic here, or overnight at one of the campsites on either side of the side creek (there's a pit toilet near the footbridge, too).

About 1 mile east of Oakridge on State 58, turn south at the sign to Kitson Springs Road. Drive 0.5 mile and turn right onto Forest Road 21, crossing the Middle Fork of the Willamette, then bearing left with the main road and continuing 3.4 miles to the Larison Cove trailhead parking area, on your right.

The narrow trail is becoming popular with mountain bikers; particularly if you see the telltale car racks in the parking area, watch carefully for bikers while hiking. Just past the trailhead, a couple of spurs lead to the water's edge; keep them in mind for cooling off on the return, though the muddy lake bottom and slight drop-off make these less-than-ideal swimming spots. Continuing up the trail, watch for poison oak.

At about 0.5 mile, the trail leads a short distance up a cool side-creek canyon to cross the creek on a railed log bridge. The trail then returns to the shoreline, usually staying about 50 feet above the water. The trailside

Creek crossing on Larison Cove Trail

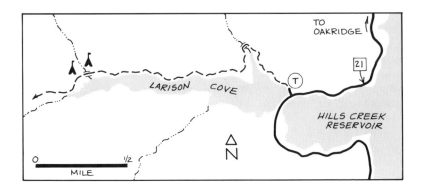

Douglas firs, cedars, hemlocks, and maples offer shade much of the way, though open stretches can be hot in summer.

At 2 miles, the trail passes a campsite shortly before reaching a second footbridge crossing another side creek. A second campsite is just across the creek. The head of the cove, where the reservoir ends and Larison Creek begins, is about 0.2 mile beyond the footbridge, for hikers interested in more exploring. Eventually the Forest Service hopes to construct a trail on the cove's south side, allowing hikers to make a loop of about 4 miles.

47. Salt Creek Falls—
Diamond Creek Falls Loop

Type:	Dayhike
Difficulty:	Easy to moderate
Distance:	3.25 miles, loop
Hikable:	June through October
Use:	Heavy
High point:	4000 feet
Elevation gain:	450 feet
Maps:	USGS Diamond Peak;
	Willamette National Forest

This loop hike begins and ends at one of the Northwest's most impressive waterfalls and includes yet another dramatic falls at the loop's far end. It's a fun trail with a lot of interesting stops along the way, including a visit to a lake named Too Much Bear—kids can have fun speculating on the origin of that name! With so many rhododendrons, June is a particularly nice month for this hike.

From Oakridge, drive southeast on State 58 about 24 miles. About 1 mile after passing through a tunnel, make a sharp right on Road 5893 and follow it a short distance to Salt Creek Falls picnic area.

Begin the outing with a walk down a short, paved path to view 286-foot Salt Creek Falls, which begins as a slide down a 50-foot cliff and ends with a dramatic free fall. Back at the picnic area, follow the paved path upstream a short distance to a footbridge crossing Salt Creek, then bear right. In about 50 yards signs indicate the start of the loop trail. Head counterclockwise (on Diamond Creek Falls Trail) to start the hike with a glimpse into Salt Creek Canyon from the other side of the creek.

After a short climb, the trail reaches a viewpoint atop a cliff of basalt columns; the columns create a cobblestonelike surface, kind of interesting (and a little treacherous) for kids, given the sheer drop-off. Too Much Bear Lake lies just down the trail, off to the left; it's a small, oval, shallow, stagnant pond ripe with potential for shoreline biological investigations.

A signed viewpoint at 0.3 mile leads to a view of the highway tunnel and sinuous creek canyon. The trail continues to roll through a forest of rhododendrons to a "viewpoint" at Lower Diamond Creek Falls at 0.7 mile. Trees obscure the view of this 200-foot falls, but this is the best view possible from the trail (though children will hear its roar as they approach and pass above it, at about 1 mile).

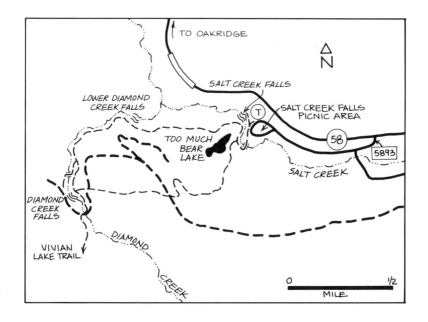

Staircase on Diamond Creek Falls spur trail

Continue up gurgling Diamond Creek, passing a couple of clearcuts filled with rhododendrons. The trail steepens for about 0.2 mile just before, 1.4 miles from the trailhead, it reaches the spur trail to Diamond Creek Falls. Follow this a short distance into the canyon, down a notched-log staircase, over a wide log bridge across the creek, and around the corner to see the 80-foot falls.

Back on the main trail, continue 0.2 mile to the junction with Vivian Lake Trail and bear left. Immediately cross a gravel road. From the junction, the trail mostly climbs gently for about 0.5 mile, then starts dropping through the forest of Douglas fir, hemlock, and lots of rhododendrons, crossing the road once again. It ends back at the lower junction with Diamond Creek Falls Trail, about 1.2 miles from the upper trail junction. Continue back across Salt Creek to the picnic area.

48. Marilyn Lakes

Type:	Dayhike
Difficulty:	Easy
Distance:	1.25 miles one way
Hikable:	July through October
Use:	Light
High point:	5000 feet
Elevation gain:	200 feet
Maps:	USGS Willamette Pass and Waldo Lake; Waldo Lake Wilderness

Two sister lakes make a fine destination for a short hike with young children. If camping at Gold Lake, hikers can walk from the campsite. Otherwise, start from either of two trailheads and walk to one or both lakes—as you wish.

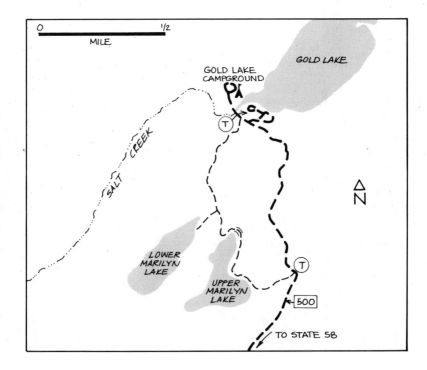

From Oakridge, take State 58 southeast 25 miles to gravel Gold Lake Road (Road 500). Follow it 1.2 miles to the lower trailhead, on the left. The upper trailhead is 0.8 mile farther, at Gold Lake Campground.

From the lower trailhead, Upper Marilyn Lake is just 0.25 mile down the trail through lush forest. The shore isn't particularly accessible at this end, although it's sunny and grassy and looks inviting for picnics. The trail gets very close to the shore as it continues around the lake's east side.

At 0.5 mile, cross a short puncheon bridge over a bog. The trail veers away from the lake, then into the woods, and hits a junction at 0.75 mile. Go left to Lower Marilyn Lake, about 150 yards away, or right to Gold Lake, 0.5 mile farther through airy woods.

There's a campsite at Upper Marilyn Lake and what looks like the beginning of a trail around the lake, but it peters out quickly. Bushwhackers in the group might have fun pushing farther around the lake.

Upper Marilyn Lake

49. Bobby Lake

Type:	Dayhike or backpack
Difficulty:	Easy to moderate
Distance:	4.6 miles round-trip
Hikable:	July through October
Use:	Light
High point:	5600 feet
Elevation gain:	100 feet
Maps:	USGS Waldo Lake and Twin Lakes; Waldo Lake Wilderness

Bobby Lake is one of dozens of lakes dotting the forest around Waldo Lake. The hike in is nearly level, though rather uneventful, and the good-size lake offers fine swimming and even decent fishing. Try to get in by late morning to soak up some sun on the big rock slab tilting into the lake's west end. The final 0.25 mile to Bobby Lake follows a chunk of the Pacific Crest Trail; families may even meet up with some long-distance trekkers who might share some of their experiences with the children.

From Oakridge, take State 58 southeast 22 miles and turn north onto Waldo Lake Road (Road 5897). Follow it 5.5 miles to a wide turnout on the left.

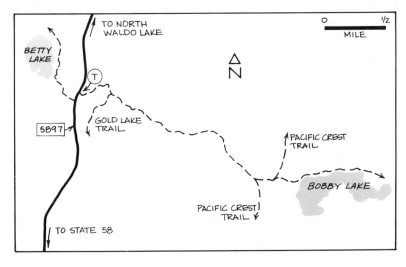

Bobby Lake

The route to Bobby Lake begins across the road on a wide trail through airy woods; it's flat or gently rolling the entire route. At 0.4 mile it arrives at a junction with Gold Lake Trail; go straight. The trail continues its fairly straight route, without many distractions, to its junction with the PCT at 2 miles. Turn left; the lake is ahead 0.3 mile. Bear right at a fork to get right to the lake; continue around to the right to get to the big rock. Otherwise, the trail continues along the lake's north shore and on into Deschutes National Forest.

Back at the trailhead, any hikers needing to work off more energy can continue across the road and stroll over to pretty Betty Lake, 0.4 mile west of the road.

50. South Waldo Shelter

Type:	Dayhike or backpack
Difficulty:	Easy
Distance:	3.4 miles round-trip
Hikable:	July through October
Use:	Light
High point:	5400 feet
Elevation gain:	Negligible
Maps:	USGS Waldo Lake;
	Waldo Lake Wilderness

At 10 square miles, Waldo Lake is the second-largest lake in Oregon and is considered one of the clearest and purest lakes in the world. It's a grand place in late summer, when the swarms of mosquitoes that plague campers earlier in the season are gone. A 21.8-mile trail encircles the entire lake; this short, level stretch offers excellent views of the lake and nice camping opportunities.

From Oakridge, take State 58 southeast 22 miles to Waldo Lake Road (Road 5897). Drive 7 miles, turn left on Road 5896 at the sign to Shadow

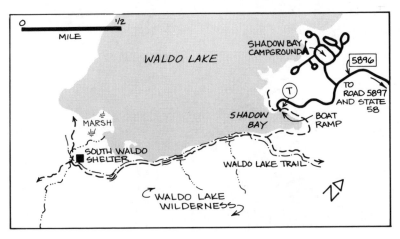

Bay Campground, and follow signs to the boat ramp.

A trail sign points toward the bay, where a mini–Waikiki Beach—a crescent of smooth, white sand—beckons. If hikers can tear themselves away, pick up the trail heading south, following it around Shadow Bay and crossing a couple of small bridges in the process. At 0.4 mile the trail joins the main Waldo Lake Trail and, shortly thereafter, enters Waldo Lake Wilderness.

About this point, pause to see if anything seems different. It should; the trail is now beyond the protection of the bay, and even on a gentle day, hikers should be feeling the wind across the lake and seeing waves lapping at the shore. Soon the trail crosses a rather substantial footbridge, then leads through a bog filled with skunk cabbage, and, at 1 mile, crosses another beefy bridge, and then another.

Here look for a particularly pretty beach; on hot summer days, its gentle surf is reminiscent of a tropical beach—a great place to play "shipwrecked!" Eventually the terrain becomes more rolling, and at about

South Waldo Shelter

1.3 miles the trail swings out of sight of the lake to skirt the marsh here. Cross one more big footbridge before reaching three-sided, shingle-roofed South Waldo Shelter at 1.7 miles.

The meadows here are inviting for camping, and the shelter itself might be a godsend on a rainy day. There are no bunks or stove, but there's a fireplace in front. Turn around here, or continue farther up the trail; Waldo Lake comes back into view in about 0.3 mile.

51. Islet Beach

Type: Dayhike
Difficulty: Easy
Distance: 2.5 miles round-trip
Hikable: July through October
Use: Light
High point: 5400 feet
Elevation gain: Negligible
Maps: USGS Waldo Lake;
Waldo Lake Wilderness

Waldo Lake offers several swimming beaches accessible by road; you must hike (or boat) to Islet Beach, and it's worth every step. A long, wide crescent of soft sand faces west and is bathed in sun all afternoon long. The hike is an easy stroll through the woods, past several smaller beaches

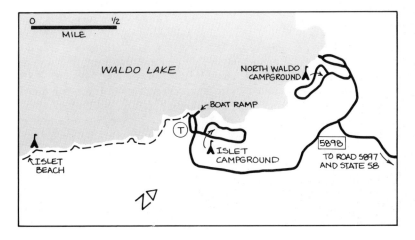

and coves—warm-up acts to the main event.

From Oakridge, take State 58 southeast 22 miles to the start of Waldo Lake Road (Road 5897); drive 13 miles (becomes Road 5898) and turn left at the sign to Islet Campground. Follow signs 1.2 miles to the boat ramp and look for the trail sign.

From the trailhead, hike south on the shoreline trail. (The main Waldo Lake Trail is some distance from the lake at this point.) Immediately the trail passes a small gray-sand beach, then a small cove at 0.2 mile, then another small beach at 0.9 mile. The kids may want to explore these coves with some thoroughness, though due to the lake's purity, they won't find many slimy, creepy, crawling, oozy life forms along the shore.

The trail ends at Islet Beach, some 75 sandy yards long. Look for a campsite on a promontory overlooking the lake just north of the beach.

52. Rigdon Lakes

Type: Dayhike (backpacking not recommended)
Difficulty: Moderate
Distance: 4.8 miles round-trip
Hikable: July through October
Use: Heavy
High point: 5500 feet
Elevation gain: 200 feet
Maps: USGS Waldo Mountain; Waldo Lake Wilderness

The hike into Ridgon Lakes is nearly level, and a couple of trailside ponds help tick off the miles as well as provide an excuse to pause for some exploring. With a boat, more than 1.5 miles could be cut off the hike by sailing or canoeing to an unmarked cove on the north shore, directly south of the junction of Waldo Lake Trail and Ridgon Lakes Trail. Bushwhack or follow game trails the 200 yards from shore to trail.

From the turn-off to Waldo Lake from State 58 (see Hike 50, South Waldo Shelter), drive 13 miles and turn right at the sign to North Waldo Campground. Continue 0.8 mile, following signs to the boating and swimming area at North Waldo. The trail begins off the lower end of the parking area, near the toilets.

From the trailhead, walk 0.1 mile before another Waldo Lake Trail comes in from the right, then bear right as the shoreline trail veers off

Upper Rigdon Lake

to the left. The trail rolls through the mountain hemlock forest, which effectively blocks any view of Waldo Lake. At 1 mile, notice the small pond—or, later in the season, marsh—on your right; it marks the halfway point to the first Rigdon Lake. Soon the trail passes another big pond on the left and a smaller one on the right. At 1.7 mile, the trail for Rigdon Lakes takes off to the right (the main trail continues around the lake).

From the junction, walk 0.3 mile to an unsigned fork; bear left to reach Upper Rigdon Lake in a few steps. Approach quietly; some birds might be seen resting on the lake. The lake is pretty, but the shoreline isn't terribly inviting; return to the main trail and continue another 0.4 mile to Lower Rigdon Lake. Its shoreline isn't much flatter, but it is shallow around the edge, inviting kids with "river shoes" (old sneakers or new water shoes) to wade in and try catching water skeeter bugs and other shoreline critters.

It's not far to a third lake, Kiwa, in case a 4.8-mile round trip isn't

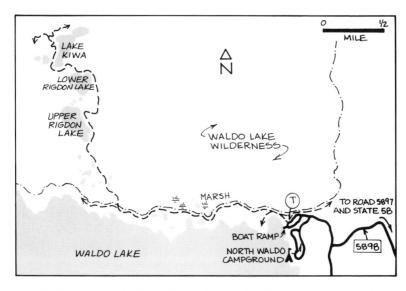

enough for your party. Camping isn't permitted within 100 feet of any of the three lakes; consider camping at North Waldo Campground and dayhiking into these lakes.

53. Rosary Lakes

Type:	Dayhike or backpack
Difficulty:	Moderate to difficult
Distance:	7 miles round-trip
Hikable:	June through October
Use:	Heavy
High point:	5880 feet
Elevation gain:	800 feet
Maps:	USGS Willamette Pass and Odell Lake; Deschutes National Forest

Rosary Lakes are what they sound like: a succession of three emerald lakes strung close together in deep forest. The most difficult part of the hike is the initial 2.7 miles to the first lake; it's not steep, just not terribly interesting. Keep children engaged with songs, or with challenging them

Middle Rosary Lake

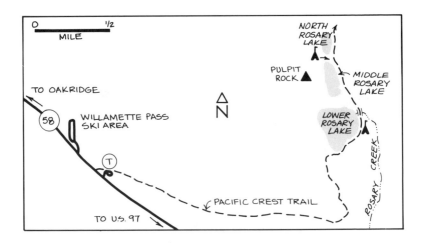

to spot Odell Lake through the trees to the south. If they're old enough to handle a hike this long, they'll be glad they did; the closely set lakes are fun for brisk dips and even trout fishing. Carry river shoes to wear into the muddy lakes.

Just past Willamette Pass ski area on State 58 (about 29 miles southeast of Oakridge), turn left at the small hiker sign. Bear right at the highway maintenance shed and gravel pit and park at the far end of the parking area, where the trail begins.

The route follows the Pacific Crest Trail through an airy pine-and-fir forest on a gentle, but steady, incline for 2.7 miles before sneaking up on Lower Rosary Lake, a medium-size mountain lake with a scree slope on its far side. The trail continues around the lake's gentle south shore, passing a number of campsites on a flat above the lake.

At 3 miles, cross a bridge over the lower lake's outlet, then start uphill toward Middle Rosary, about 0.4 mile farther. North Rosary is at 3.5 miles, just across a narrow band of forest from its sister.

North Umpqua River

State 138

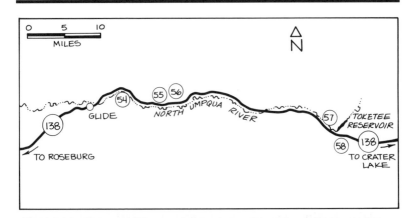

Wild iris, Fall Creek Falls

54. Lower North Umpqua Trail: Fern Falls

Type: Dayhike
Difficulty: Easy
Distance: 3.5 miles round-trip
Hikable: Year-round
Use: Light
Elevation: 840 feet
Elevation gain: Negligible
Maps: USGS Glide and Fairview;
USFS and BLM North Umpqua
Trail brochure

Another of western Oregon's classic riverside trails, the North Umpqua Trail runs some 76 miles from Swiftwater Bridge, 21 miles east of Roseburg, to the Pacific Crest Trail in Mount Thielson Wilderness. Though portions of the trail are still under construction, the lower 26.2 miles is completed and is particularly appealing to families, as it provides year-round hiking opportunities on gentle grades. Here the trail follows the river's south bank, opposite State 138; road bridges at four points naturally divide the trail into three sections ranging from 5 to 15.7 miles in length.

The lowest section is a long one, too long for a day hike. However, it lends itself to an out-and-back hike to Fern Falls that's accessible all

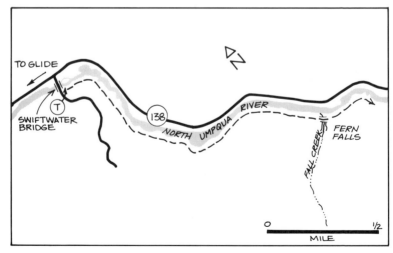

Fern Falls

year. Try other trail sections as time and curiosity lead you. Each section has its own rewards; maps detailing the entire trail as well as trail guides describing each section are available from local Forest Service and BLM offices.

From Glide (15 miles east of Roseburg), drive east 6 miles on State 138 to Swiftwater Bridge, on the right. The trail starts just across the bridge on the upstream side. (The next access point is in 15.7 miles, at Wright Creek Bridge.)

From Swiftwater Bridge, hike up the nearly level trail, traversing a gorgeous forest dripping with moss. The trail crosses little side creeks, and there are numerous opportunities to scramble down to the rushing North Umpqua. Stay on the lookout for poison oak all along the trail.

At 1.75 miles the trail crosses Fall Creek (not the same Fall Creek as in Hike 56) on a laminated wood footbridge at Fern Falls. Under the bridge, the creek spreads out in a shallow, rocky fan inviting for water play. Continue up the trail, or turn around and return the way you came.

55. Susan Creek Falls

Type: Dayhike
Difficulty: Easy
Distance: 1 mile round-trip
Hikable: Year-round
Use: Heavy
High point: 1060 feet
Elevation gain: 120 feet
Map: USGS Mace Mountain

The North Umpqua corridor is blessed with a wealth of short waterfall hikes, ideal for families with young children. Rather than plan a single long hike, why not spend a day driving up State 138, stopping to take in two or three short hikes? If this sounds appealing, consider Susan Creek Falls as one stop; the trail is only a half-hour's drive from Roseburg, and its low elevation means spring and its wildflowers come early.

From Glide, take State 138 east 12 miles to the Susan Creek Falls trailhead. The trail is on the north side of the highway, but parking is

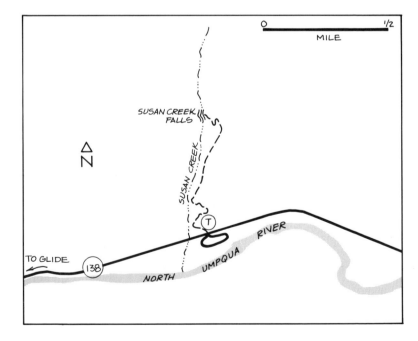

Cooling toes in Susan Creek

on the south, in a BLM picnic area.

Follow the trail through deep forest east of the creek. The trail ends at the base of the falls, which tumbles 60 feet into a punch bowl. Encourage children to look for dippers, or water ouzels—small, dark-gray birds adapted to life in and around mountain streams. They often build nests right on the edge of waterfalls, and they're frequently seen at Susan Creek Falls dipping in the spray and walking under the stream.

Fall Creek Falls

56. Fall Creek Falls

Type: Dayhike
Difficulty: Easy
Distance: 1.8 miles round-trip
Hikable: Year-round
Use: Heavy
High point: 1400 feet
Elevation gain: 380 feet
Maps: USGS Mace Mountain;
Umpqua National Forest

It's easy to keep kids interested all the way along this short trail, from the wooden bridge at the trailhead to the viewing platform part way up the falls. Spring brings an array of woodland wildflowers to the trail's borders, further enhancing a hike here.

From Glide, drive east 16.5 miles on State 138 to the signed trailhead parking lot, on the left.

From the trailhead, immediately cross Fall Creek on a wooden bridge, then pass through a cut in a tree that appears to have fallen across the trail—a perfect opportunity to talk about assessing a tree's age from the rings in the stump. (If children are overwhelmed by the number of rings, look for the rings indicating the years they were born.)

Just up the trail, squeeze through a crevice in a rock the size of a small house. The trail continues close to the creek, which spills and

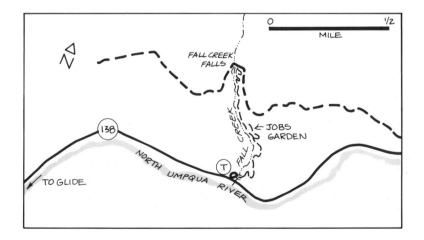

froths over mossy boulders. It switchbacks uphill briefly; then, at about 0.5 mile, a spur trail takes off to the right, leading to Jobs Garden (an area of unusual rock formations) in 0.1 mile. There's plenty of poison oak here, so be watchful and stay on the trail. As the creek flattens, the trail levels out and veers away from it, still staying in earshot.

At about 0.8 mile the trail rejoins the creek, now flat and quiet, just before reaching the falls. Here the creek twists around a corner, then showers down a rock face, falling nearly 100 feet in the process. A slippery log crosses the creek just downstream of the falls—fun to walk on, but hazardous without close supervision.

The trail continues up the hill next to the falls, switchbacking four more times to the top of the falls. It's a fun way to work off a little extra energy, but there's not much to see at the top, though there's a nice intermediate viewpoint along the way. The trail ends at a gravel road atop the falls.

57. Toketee Falls

Type:	Dayhike
Difficulty:	Easy
Distance:	0.8 mile round-trip
Hikable:	Most of the year
Use:	Heavy
High point:	2360 feet
Elevation gain:	100 feet
Maps:	USGS Toketee Falls;
	Umpqua National Forest

Toketee Falls is probably the most dramatic of the North Umpqua corridor falls, especially viewed as hikers do—across a chasm from a platform clinging to a cliff. Children will enjoy watching the water burble and swirl in the creek alongside the trail as it approaches the falls. The narrow tread and steep drop-offs urge caution with young children, however. (The trail is scheduled for reconstruction by 1996.)

From Glide, drive east on State 138 about 40 miles and turn north at the west entrance to Toketee Ranger Station. Turn left, cross a bridge, then turn left again and drive a short distance to the trailhead.

From the parking area, cross a footbridge and walk the level path through the forest, passing several potential picnic sites along the river. The trail then starts to climb a bit, becoming rocky in places. Peek down

Toketee Falls, from viewing platform

to the left to the gorgeous deep pools in the creek along the trail. The group may want to wander off the trail to play in a safe spot along the creek.

Approaching the end, the trail drops about 100 feet to a viewing platform perched on the side of the canyon. Look across a wide gulf to see the North Umpqua River pouring through a cleft in a wall of columnar basalt and dropping some 90 feet into an emerald pool.

Children will no doubt be curious about the huge redwood "pipe"

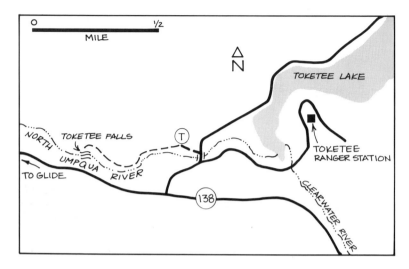

oozing water in a few places next to the trailhead. It diverts water from nearby Toketee Lake and carries it to another pipe, where it drops steeply to a powerhouse to make electricity.

58. Watson Falls

Type:	Dayhike
Difficulty:	Easy
Distance:	1 mile round-trip
Hikable:	Most of the year
Use:	Heavy
High point:	3040 feet
Elevation gain:	280 feet
Maps:	USGS Fish Creek Desert; Umpqua National Forest

What's fun about this, another of the North Umpqua short waterfall hikes, is the way the trail follows the steep, crashing creek up to a series of wooden viewing platforms at 272-foot Watson Falls. The climb is rather steep, but views of the falls easily tease even reluctant hikers all the way to the top.

From Glide, drive east on State 138 about 42 miles and turn right onto Road 37. Park in the large, signed parking area on the north side of the highway.

From the parking area, the signed trail leads up across Road 37 and onto a footpath ascending the hillside across the road. The route is rather steep, sticking close to the creek as it runs noisily over mossy boulders down out of the mountains. The first falls view comes at about 0.25 mile.

Watson Falls

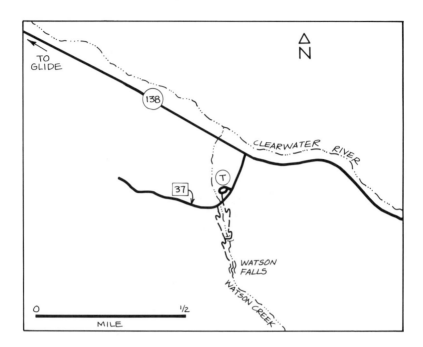

Keep going to a railed wooden platform zigzagging over the creek near the base of the falls.

Continue up the trail on another switchback for a better view of the falls, then up yet another switchback to reach the highest viewpoint, poised about one-third of the way up the falls in a magnificent natural amphitheater of gray and pale green rock and moss. The cataract falls straight down a cliff, like a mini-Multnomah Falls, pounding a pile of boulders and vaporizing into clouds of mist.

To return, follow signs to the "return trail" spur that starts just east of the railed platform bridge. It takes a slightly steeper, quicker route back to the parking area.

Crater Lake and Upper Rogue River

State 62 and 230

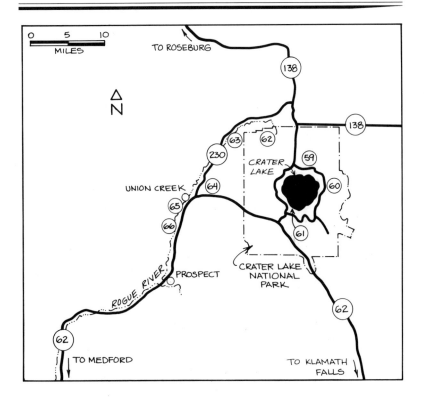

59. Cleetwood Cove

Type: Dayhike
Difficulty: Moderate
Distance: 2.2 miles round-trip
Hikable: July through September
Use: Heavy
High point: 6935 feet
Elevation gain: 760 feet
Map: USGS Crater Lake National Park and Vicinity

Thousands of people drive around the rim of Crater Lake, gazing across its deep, clear blue waters, but far fewer actually dip their toes in it. There's only one way to get to the lake, and that's a hike down the Cleetwood Trail. Boat tours out to Wizard Island leave from the dock at the trail's end; check at park headquarters for the schedule. Even without the boat ride, the hike is worthwhile; how many other kids do the kids know who have swum in Crater Lake?

 From the park's western border (70 miles northeast of Medford), continue east about 7 miles on State 62 and turn left toward park headquarters. In 4 miles, turn left on Rim Drive and drive 3 miles to Rim Village. The trailhead is almost directly across the lake from Rim Village; if driving, go clockwise around the rim road 10.6 miles. Park across the road from the trailhead in the large parking area.

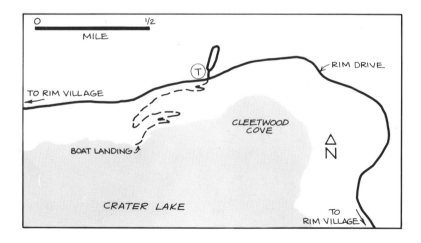

The wide trail's descent isn't really steep, but it's steady. Benches are scattered all along the trail. (The prospect of a boat tour motivates lots of less-than-fit tourists to walk this trail; they make good use of the opportunities to rest.) The lake glimmers along the trail all the way down the long switchbacks.

The trail ends at the little boat dock. Sit on the edge of the dock, dipping your feet, or pick your way along the bouldery shore to find a picnic or wading spot. Carry river tennies for wading, as the rocks can be sharp. It's a perfect opportunity to talk with kids about geologic time and the relative youth of a mountain like Mount Mazama.

Dock at Cleetwood Cove, on Crater Lake

60. Mount Scott

Type: Dayhike
Difficulty: Difficult
Distance: 5 miles round-trip
Hikable: July through September
Use: Light
High point: 8926 feet
Elevation gain: 1326 feet
Map: USGS Crater Lake National Park
and Vicinity

With the elevation gain, distance, and lung-stretching height of the peak, an ascent of Mount Scott is a challenge. Those who make it are rewarded with the ultimate view of Crater Lake, from the highest point in the national park, as well as views of the Three Sisters to the north, Mount Shasta to the south, and many peaks in between. There's a lookout cabin at the top; it's usually occupied in August and September, when fire danger is highest.

For road directions to Rim Village, see Hike 59, Cleetwood Cove. From Rim Village, the trailhead for Mount Scott is about 18 miles around Rim Drive, whether you drive clockwise or counterclockwise. Park in the turnout along the road. A large sign marks the start of the trail and provides

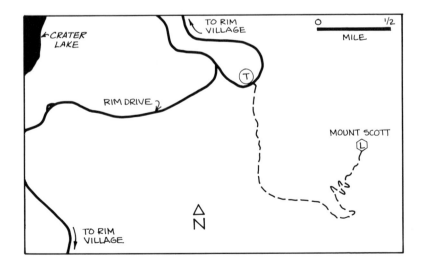

Crater Lake from summit of Mount Scott

information on the peak's geological history.

Follow the trail around the edge of a grassy cirque, then into the trees, where the trail starts its steady ascent. At 0.5 mile the trail emerges from the trees and remains fairly exposed the rest of the way up. After curving well around the mountain's south flank, the trail switchbacks at 1.5 miles and heads in the other direction to 1.8 miles, then starts a series of shorter switchbacks that end on the summit ridge. From there it's a short walk to the lookout perched on the tiptop. A map will help identify the peaks that can be seen if the weather is clear. The drop is pretty precipitous from the top; take care with footing and the children's exploring. If the ladder to the lookout is down, it might be possible to visit with the ranger on duty.

61. Garfield Peak

Type: Dayhike
Difficulty: Moderate
Distance: 3 miles round-trip
Hikable: July through September
Use: Heavy
High point: 8060 feet
Elevation gain: 980 feet
Map: USGS Crater Lake National Park
and Vicinity

You can get perfectly wonderful views of Crater Lake from the rim road, but for even more wonderful views, do a little hiking. The hike up Garfield Peak is the easier of two summit trails in the park; it starts just east of the old lodge in Rim Village, making it easily accessible for those just passing through the park following the west rim and not planning to drive the entire Rim Drive.

For road directions to Rim Village, see Hike 59, Cleetwood Cove. Park in the Rim Village area, on the crater's southwest edge, and walk back behind Crater Lake Lodge, slated for reconstruction in the mid-1990s. Follow the asphalt path along the masonry wall at the rim, drinking in views of the lake and Wizard Island. The trail starts up the mountain, reaching a bench for resting at 0.25 mile. Here the trail turns away from the lake and starts traversing along the peak's southern slope. Your back is to the lake much of the way; to help kids along, try urging them to

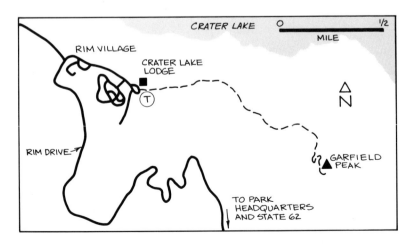

Snow-dusted Garfield Peak

walk five minutes between peeks, helping them gauge their progress. If it seems like more than 1.5 miles to the top, remind kids that the elevation is quite high and their bodies probably haven't had enough time to adjust to working with less oxygen.

Toward the end, the trail switchbacks a few turns to reach the summit. In contrast to Mount Scott, the summit is quite large and flat and relatively safe with children.

62. Boundary Springs

Type:	Dayhike
Difficulty:	Moderate
Distance:	5 miles round-trip
Hikable:	June through October
Use:	Light
High point:	5060 feet
Elevation gain:	310 feet
Maps:	USGS Pumice Desert West;
	Rogue River National Forest

People who visit Boundary Springs invariably talk about it in mystical terms: it's enchanting to some, spiritual to others. It's hard not to be awed watching a river emerge whole from a hillside of mossy springs.

Upper Rogue River from trail to Boundary Springs

While most rivers have their beginnings in little creeks that slowly merge with other little creeks, then with bigger creeks, the Rogue River is too big to jump across from the moment it's born on the slopes below Crater Lake. If the children have ever rafted, waded, fished, or swum in the Rogue, the hike into its headwaters will have special significance.

From its junction with State 62 north of Union Creek, follow State 230 northeast 18 miles to the trailhead at Crater Rim Viewpoint, and park. From the parking lot, follow the Upper Rogue River Trail down to a flat lodgepole forest and walk through it for 0.5 mile, bearing left at the junction with Boundary Springs Trail.

Follow the trail along a bench above the Rogue for another 0.25 mile, until the trail emerges from the woods at Road 760. (It's also possible to drive to this point along Road 760, a rather slow-going dirt road; the ranger station in Prospect has directions.) Cross the road (and the Rogue) on the road bridge and pick up the trail again.

From here the trail follows along the river, generally in sight of it but well above it. From Road 760, it's about 0.75 mile to the signed entrance to Crater Lake National Park and another 0.75 mile to Boundary Springs. You'll know you're at the springs from the lushness of the surrounding woods. The main trail fades as spur routes lead hither and yon through the springs area. Urge children to respect the delicate

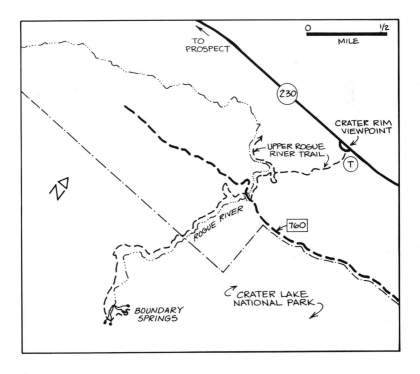

environment here, staying off the moss carpet, and to take care on slippery logs and rocks. Mosquitoes can be plentiful, especially in June and July. To further protect the area, don't camp near the springs.

63. National Creek Falls

Type:	Dayhike
Difficulty:	Easy
Distance:	0.8 miles round-trip
Hikable:	May through October
Use:	Light
High point:	4000 feet
Elevation gain:	160 feet
Maps:	USGS Hamaker Butte;
	Rogue River National Forest

In summer, National Creek Falls is a wonderfully cool retreat at the end of an easy hike, a good choice for families camping in the area. Waves of mist assault hikers approaching the falls; along the way, wildflowers (peaking around late May) give the trail a fairyland feel.

From Union Creek, drive north 1.3 miles on State 62, bearing left onto State 230 and continuing 6 miles. Turn right onto Forest Road 6530 and

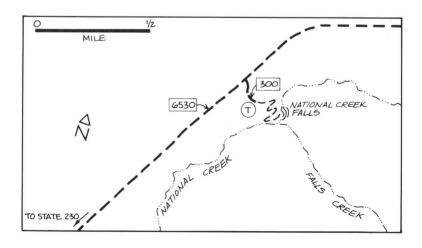

National Creek Falls

drive 3.7 miles (bearing left at the junction with Road 6535), turn right onto Road 300, and continue a short distance to the trailhead.

The trail switchbacks gently down the hillside 0.2 mile to reach the top of the falls. Continue another 0.2 mile down into the steep-walled canyon to the base of the falls, through a forest of Douglas fir, pine, and hemlock. (How many different kinds of cones can the kids find along the trail?) Near the bottom of the trail, look for an uprooted tree nursing a miniforest of young conifers.

64. Union Creek

Type: Dayhike
Difficulty: Easy to moderate
Distance: 4 miles one way
Hikable: May through October
Use: Heavy
High point: 3765 feet
Elevation gain or loss: 445 feet
Maps: USGS Union Creek;
Rogue River National Forest

Union Creek is the kind of trail that sneaks up on you. There are no dramatic vistas, just easy walking through a magnificent forest following a babbling creek. Start a one-way hike at the upper end with a splash (a view of pretty Union Falls) and end at the community of Union Creek, or begin at Union Creek and wander upstream a mile or two, then turn around. In addition to huge, old-growth Douglas fir, there are hemlocks, sugar pines, alder, yew, and all kinds of wildflowers in late spring.

The lower trailhead is on the south side of the highway bridge over the creek at the community of Union Creek, which is 11 miles north of Prospect on State 62. Follow the path up the east bank a short distance, cross the creek on a footbridge (slippery when wet), and continue up the west bank.

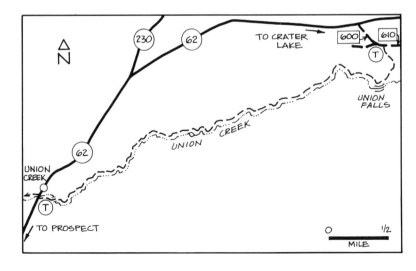

Old growth along Union Creek Trail

To reach the upper trailhead, continue north from the community of Union Creek 3.3 miles on State 62 and turn right onto Road 600 at the sign to the Union Creek trailhead. Go 0.2 mile and bear left onto Road 610; the trailhead is on the right in 0.2 mile.

From the upper trailhead, walk through the level forest, listening for falls, then drop down the hillside to reach the base of Union Falls at 0.3 mile. Here the creek drops about 5 feet over a smooth lip, then churns and boils down several more ledges.

From the falls, the trail winds gently down along the west bank, usually in sight of the wide creek. Notice the moss-covered volcanic creekbed at the upper end; farther down, as the lava diminishes, the creek's edges are less well defined. Logs are strewn across the creek in many places, creating tempting footbridges and obscuring the creek in places. Point out to children the islands midstream; some appear to have started after a tree fell into the creek and other plants began to grow on the decaying tree. They can also see dry channels where the creek was apparently diverted by a logjam. What caused all those logs to fall into the creek? Let the kids think about it—then suggest a few options: logging operations, beavers, wind, and even the creek itself, undercutting the root systems of trees along its bank.

After crossing the footbridge back at Union Creek, the trail reaches the highway at 4 miles, but it continues across the road another 0.4 mile to intersect the Rogue Gorge Trail. You'll want to visit Rogue Gorge while you're in the area; a short asphalt path leads past dramatic views of the Rogue River churning its way through a narrow lava chasm. Fencing and viewing platforms make it safe for children.

65. Natural Bridge Loop

Type:	Dayhike
Difficulty:	Easy
Distance:	2 miles, loop
Hikable:	May through October
Use:	Light
High point:	3200 feet
Elevation gain:	200 feet
Maps:	USGS Union Creek;
	Rogue River National Forest

In its dash from the slopes of Mount Mazama, holding Crater Lake, to the Pacific Ocean, the Rogue River does a sudden disappearing act, reappearing a short distance downstream. Where did it go? Into a series of lava tubes in the river's channel. The Forest Service has developed an excellent interpretive trail overlooking Natural Bridge that serves to

Early steps on Natural Bridge interpretive trail

enlighten visitors as well as to steer them safely away from walking on Natural Bridge itself. Link that short, paved path with forest trails on either side of the river, throw in a pair of footbridges, and what results is a wonderful, and relatively little-known, loop. The east-bank trail section skirts a busy campground, but the west-bank section is little used.

From Union Creek (11 miles north of Prospect), drive south 1 mile on State 62 and turn west at the sign to Natural Bridge onto Road 300. Continue 0.5 mile, bearing left at the Y, and park at the day-use area.

From the parking area, a paved path leads to a dramatic metal footbridge spanning the churning Rogue River. The path then winds

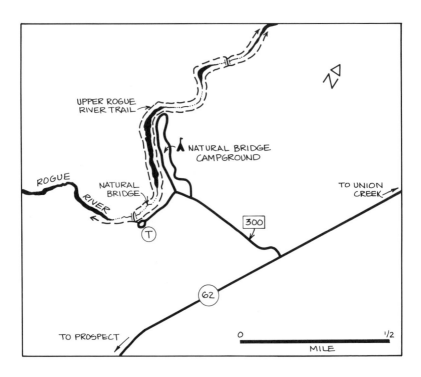

upstream, safely fenced off from steep cliffs, with several overlooks and signs explaining the geologic processes that created the scene below.

The paved path ends at a view of Natural Bridge, but the trail—Upper Rogue River Trail— continues as a dirt footpath. It follows a level course for about 0.25 mile, then climbs perhaps 200 feet above the river in deep woods. Look down and see the now peacefully flowing green river between the trees.

After a while tents and trailers can be glimpsed parked in the campground across the river; then a bright, bleached, wooden footbridge is seen below. The trail seems to overshoot the footbridge as it drops to river level, but a right turn at a trail junction leads along a quaint, rock-lined path back to the bridge. Cross it and turn right (a left turn leads 1.5 miles to Union Creek). The north end of the campground is about 0.25 mile from the bridge. The trail here threads between river and campground for 0.5 mile or so; notice the river's initial calm, then its growing sense of urgency, as it narrows and drops toward Natural Bridge. For the last 0.25 mile the trail veers away from the river and into the woods, ending at the viewpoint parking area.

The trail is generally snow-free from April through November, but the road to Natural Bridge is open only mid-May through mid-October. It's possible to walk the 0.5 mile in from the highway or, better yet, hike down 1.5 miles from Union Creek on the east-bank trail to catch the loop. You're likely to have the entire trail to yourself.

66. Takelma Gorge

Type: Dayhike
Difficulty: Easy to moderate
Distance: 4.5 miles one way
Hikable: May through October
Use: Heavy
High point: 2960 feet
Elevation gain or loss: 120 feet
Maps: USGS Prospect North and Whetstone Point; Rogue River National Forest

The 48-mile-long Upper Rogue River Trail follows the river from the town of Prospect upstream to Crater Rim Viewpoint, just outside Crater Lake National Park, providing lots of options for relatively easy one-way and round-trip hikes. Two of those options appear in this book: Hike 65 (Natural Bridge Loop) and this one, a hike to dramatic Takelma Gorge. With a shuttle car, a 4.5-mile one-way hike is possible; otherwise, it's 3 miles round-trip from Woodruff Bridge to the gorge and back.

From Union Creek, drive 4.7 miles south on State 62 and turn right at the sign to Woodruff Bridge onto Road 68. Continue 2 miles and park on the left just before the bridge.

From the parking area, head south on Upper Rogue River Trail, stopping to fill water bottles at an old-fashioned water pump. The trail continues 0.25 mile before the river can be seen again, flowing placidly here. The trail continues downstream, mostly level with a few ups and downs, with the river mostly out of sight.

At about 1 mile, the river can be heard and seen quickening its pace, as if it were anticipating the gorge ahead. The trail grows rockier where it passes atop basalt-column cliffs; see cliffs across the river. Is this the gorge? Not quite; it's obvious when it appears. Continue another 0.4 mile and there it is: a channel of whitewater turning sharply and roaring between vertical cliffs of dark basalt, under logs swept downstream and lodged between the gorge walls.

Water pump at Takelma Gorge trailhead

Turn around, or continue along the top of the gorge for its 0.5-mile length. Below the gorge the river flattens again, and it's a mellow 2.5 miles to River Bridge Campground. To leave a car at this end, take State 62 south 2.2 miles from the Woodruff Bridge turn-off, turn right on gravel Road 6210, and follow it 1 mile to the campground.

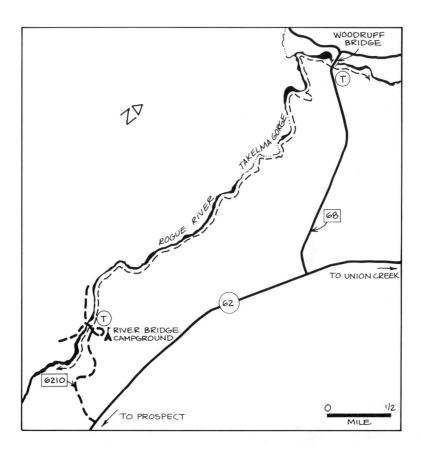

Greater Rogue Valley

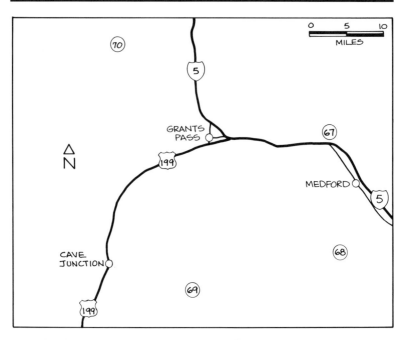

Mushroom

67. Upper Table Rock

Type:	Dayhike
Difficulty:	Moderate
Distance:	3 miles round-trip
Hikable:	Most of the year
Use:	Heavy
High point:	2050 feet
Elevation gain:	750 feet
Maps:	USGS Sams Valley;
	The Table Rocks brochure
	(BLM and The Nature
	Conservancy)

Anyone who has driven past Medford on I-5 has noticed the pair of flat-top mesas north of the freeway. Both Upper and Lower Table Rock have trails to their summits; the trail ascending Upper Table Rock is shorter, a little less steep, and a little more open for views. It's a good wildflower walk in spring, but children will be more intrigued by the summit, which is literally flat enough to land a plane on. The grassy summit is a bit boggy in winter and spring; in summer, hikers may end up with a few burrs in their socks. In all seasons, beware of poison oak— and, some say, rattlesnakes.

From I-5 in Medford, take the Central Point exit and follow Biddle Road 1 mile to Table Rock Road. Turn left and drive 5.3 miles; where

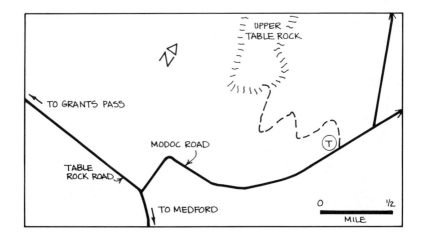

Moth on hiker's hand, on Upper Table Rock

the road swings to the left, turn right on Modoc Road and continue 1.5 miles to the signed BLM trailhead, on the left.

The trail is rocky in places, muddy in others, but generally in good shape. From the trailhead, start up through a tangle of oak and madrone trees. The trail passes between huge basalt outcrops at 0.2 mile. At 0.5 mile there's a bench inviting hikers to pause and enjoy the view of the Rogue Valley. There's a bench at 0.9 mile, where the trail enters the forest and obscures the view the rest of the way to the summit. The upper part of the trail has some steep pitches. Quite suddenly, at 1.5 miles, the trail emerges onto the flat, open expanse at the top of the rock.

Even kids who have a hard time dragging themselves to the summit tend to be irrepressible once on top, exploding in the open, virtually treeless landscape and compelled to walk or run to the clifftop at the edge of the summit. The trail hits the summit near one end of the horseshoe-shaped rock; head left to get to the end, or wander to the center of the horseshoe for a dramatic view of the rocky gorge below.

68. Sterling Mine Ditch Loop

Type: Dayhike
Difficulty: Moderate to difficult
Distance: 6.3 miles, loop
Hikable: Most of the year
Use: Heavy
High point: 2940 feet
Elevation gain: 260 feet
Maps: USGS Sterling Creek;
BLM Sterling Mine Trail
System brochure

In 1877, hundreds of Chinese laborers finished construction of a 26.5-mile-long ditch designed to carry water from the Little Applegate River to Sterling Creek, where gold had been discovered twenty-three years

Tunnel on Sterling Mine Ditch

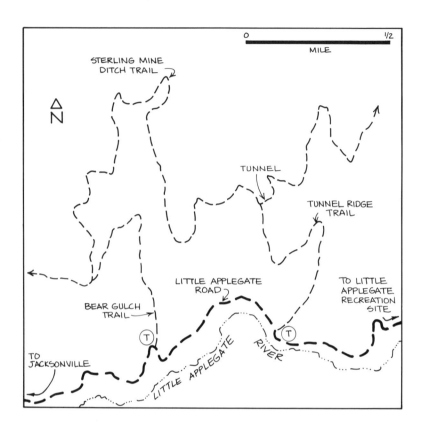

earlier. The ditch was abandoned in the 1940s, but in the late 1980s 16.6 miles of the wide berm bordering the ditch was reclaimed as a nearly level, and fairly remote, hiking, equestrian, and mountain-biking path. Three access trails lead 1 to 1.5 miles from the road to the trail, creating opportunities for loop trips.

Sterling Mine Ditch offers a completely unique hiking opportunity. The BLM's trail brochure provides more historical background as well as a plant list and map. Go in early spring, when it's not too hot and when wildflowers are in bloom, but watch carefully for poison oak. The loop route described here is one of several options; if a 6.3-mile hike seems too long, just walk up the Tunnel Ridge Trail to the berm, where kids can explore a tunnel and walk along the ditch a little way before turning around.

From Ruch, 7.5 miles southwest of Jacksonville, turn south off State 238 onto Little Applegate Road at the sign to Upper Applegate. Follow it 12.8 miles (turning left at the sign to Little Applegate Recreation Area at 2.9 miles) to the Tunnel Ridge trailhead. The trailhead is on the left; park in the turnout on the right.

The hike up Tunnel Ridge Trail is a steady, uphill climb on a narrow path, leading first through Douglas fir, then oak, then manzanita. At about 1 mile, the trail emerges from the trees onto an open, grassy slope with lovely vistas of the surrounding hills. Children can stay busy looking for signs of coyote and deer and for signs (hoofprints, bike tracks, bootprints) of other human trail users.

At 1.2 mile, Tunnel Ridge Trail meets the main trail right on top of a short tunnel; look for the openings a few steps to the right or left. The tunnel is narrow, but children can safely crawl through. To continue the hike, bear left on the berm snaking around the hillside. The berm is nearly level because the ditch was designed to carry water, flowing with gravity, from the Little Applegate River to Sterling Creek without losing too much elevation. Miners wanted to get the gold out of Sterling Creek, and the cheapest and most efficient way to do that was to shoot jets of water at the creekbank, where the gold was, washing the heavier gold out of layers of soil and rock. That method is called hydraulic mining.

After a pleasant 3-mile stroll westward on the berm, you'll reach the junction with Bear Gulch Trail, leading back down to the road in 1.5 miles. At the trail's end, walk back up the road 0.6 mile to your car. The road shoulders aren't very wide, but traffic is light. Nevertheless, use caution here. In summer, reward yourself with a dip in the Little Applegate River at the recreation site 2 miles farther up the road from the Tunnel Ridge trailhead.

69. Oregon Caves–Big Tree Loop

Type: Dayhike
Difficulty: Moderate
Distance: 3.3 miles, loop
Hikable: July through October
Use: Light
High point: 5080 feet
Elevation gain: 1100 feet
Maps: USGS Oregon Caves;
Oregon Caves brochure
(National Park Service)

Hikers in southern Oregon don't tend to think of the trails around Oregon Caves National Monument when choosing a destination, and tourists visiting the caves don't tend to be interested in hiking. The combination makes this interesting and moderately challenging loop trail uncrowded as well, despite its proximity to a popular tourist attraction. This hike, along with a tour of the caves, makes a full day's outing for a family. The complete loop is 3.3 miles, but an out-and-back hike to the huge Douglas fir is only 2.6 miles. Ask at the information desk about even shorter loop hikes in the caves area.

From Cave Junction, follow State 46 east 19 miles to the parking lot at Oregon Caves National Monument. Walk up the road toward the cave entrance, then continue up the double staircases, past the ticket booth and onto an asphalt path. Immediately the trail splits, signaling the start of the loop trail. Turn left for a more gradual approach to the Big Tree.

The trail quickly turns to dirt. The route is fairly steep for the first 0.4 mile, then flattens out for a bit where the first of several trailside benches appears. Then the trail makes a turn to the right; notice how the trees are bigger here and the forest cooler. At about 0.7 mile the trail gets steeper again and heads up steadily. In early July some pink rhododendrons may be in bloom. At 1.3 miles, cross a tiny creek and immediately reach the 12.5-foot-thick Douglas fir, estimated to be 1200 to 1500 years old, for which the trail is named.

From here, the trail continues up steadily another 0.4 mile to a junction; bear right and begin the descent. The trail cuts through a moist hillside where a profusion of flowers crowding the trail blooms in early summer; if the day is wet, hikers' legs will be, too.

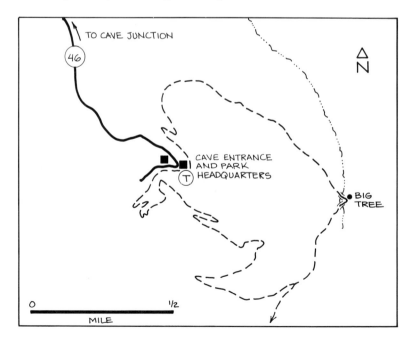

Ancient Douglas fir near Oregon Caves

Swing down through the old-growth forest on long switchbacks. Suddenly, at about 3 miles, the trail emerges from the forest to offer a view over the shake-roofed Oregon Caves buildings, silvery in sunlight. The trail passes a couple of interpretive signs before turning to asphalt for the last 0.2 mile to the caves entrance area.

70. Rogue River Trail: Grave Creek to Whiskey Creek

Type:	Dayhike or backpack
Difficulty:	Moderate to difficult
Distance:	6.6 miles round-trip
Hikable:	Most of the year
Use:	Heavy
High point:	790 feet
Elevation gain:	760 feet
Maps:	USGS Mount Reuben and Bunker Creek; USFS and BLM Wild and Scenic Rogue River

A wilderness river alternating between placid pools and wild whitewater, old cabins and archeological sites, and a benign climate are just a few of the attractions of the Rogue River Trail. It's not as level as some riverside trails, but neither is it difficult, and attractions all along the way keep children interested, as long as the hike isn't started midday in midsummer.

Late spring—May, in particular—is the ideal season to hike the Rogue River Trail. There may be some showers or even a real storm, but weather

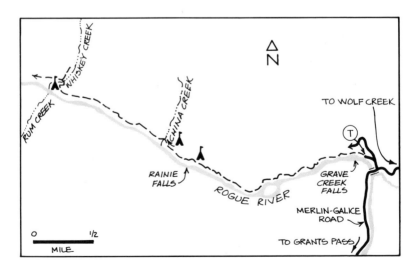

Trail marker along Rogue River

tends to be pleasantly sunny and warm, and hikers are treated to the sweet scent of wild azaleas wafting up the canyon as soon as the sun hits the pastel blossoms in midmorning. Take a week to backpack the entire trail, camping along the way, or go light and take four days to hike it lodge-to-lodge; several wilderness inns along the river cater to hikers as well as rafters and anglers.

For an easy dayhike, start at the trail's east end, near Galice outside of Grants Pass, and hike 1.8 miles down to Rainie Falls and back, or 1.5 miles farther to Whiskey Creek. There are campsites at both spots, making them attractive as destinations for easy overnighters.

From Merlin, about 5 miles north of Grants Pass, follow the Merlin—Galice Road west 25 miles, past the town of Galice, to Grave Creek Bridge over the Rogue. Cross the bridge and take the spur road to the boat landing and trailhead on the left. If planning to be out overnight, make arrangements with the Galice Resort to have your car shuttled back to Galice—it's illegal, and unwise, to leave a car at the landing overnight. There's also a trail to Rainie Falls on the river's south bank.

The trail starts up steeply, along a sheer slope overlooking the river, then levels out. At 0.6 mile look around to see the remains of an old miner's cabin. Another cabin can be seen across the river at 1.3 miles. Notice the concrete pier here; it was part of a stock bridge built in 1907 but destroyed in the flood of 1927. At 1.8 miles the trail reaches Rainie Falls, a dramatic 15-to-20-foot drop in the river. Hang around and there may be a chance to see a party of boaters use ropes to line their rafts or drift boats down the narrow, more gradual channel along the north bank. A spur trail to the camping area is 0.1 mile back upstream.

Continuing down the trail, cross China Creek at 2.1 miles. At about 2.6 miles, notice the green-black rock along the trail. The trail is crossing a fault in the earth, and this rock, called serpentine, was squeezed out to the surface here from deep in the earth. Whiskey Creek is at 3.3 miles. (Across the river is Rum Creek. What do you think those old miners who named the creeks had on their minds?) The broad meadow and beach here make it an appealing spot for a picnic and a popular spot for camping. There's another camping area 0.4 mile downstream, the last one for 2 miles.

The Forest Service map listed above is an excellent guide for hikers; it offers historical and other background information on the trail. For information on the wilderness lodges along the Rogue River, or for additional trail information, contact the Rand River Information Center, 14335 Galice Road, Merlin, OR 97532.

Greater Willamette Valley

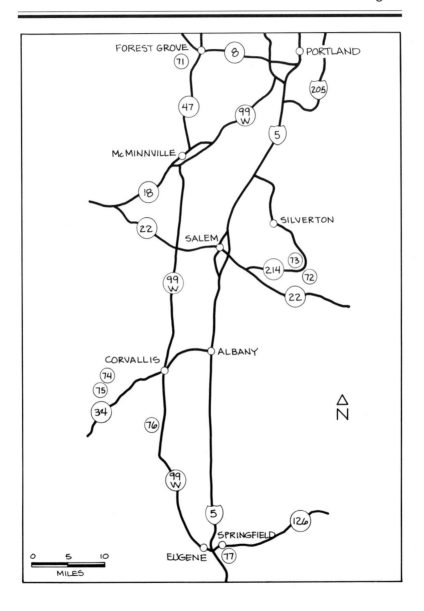

71. Hagg Lake Sampler

Type: Dayhike
Difficulty: Easy
Distance: 4 miles round-trip
Hikable: Year-round
Use: Heavy
High point: 400 feet
Elevation gain: 80 feet
Map: Henry Hagg Lake
(Bureau of Reclamation)

In summer, Henry Hagg Lake is a busy and rather noisy place. Most visitors to the reservoir come for fishing, waterskiing, picnicking, and swimming, but hikers are getting to know the 15-mile trail encircling the lake as well. Include some hiking in your next summertime visit to Hagg Lake, or make a point of hiking the lakeshore in the quiet before fishing season opens in April or in late fall after the summer rush. Just be sure to wear waterproof boots, as the trail gets pretty muddy in spots.

The trail lies close to the road much of the way around, and spur

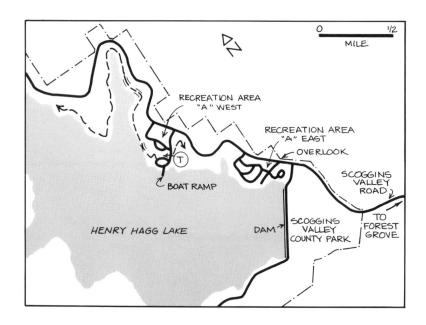

Balance practice at Hagg Lake boat ramp

trails grant access at numerous points, affording plenty of options for short dayhikes. This 2-mile stretch, along the lake's north shore, offers a variety of views and options for lakeside picnics and ends at a pleasant swimming beach. After trying this sampler, come back to try other stretches; with a shuttle car, drop one car and then drive along the road about as far as you think you want to walk and start back on foot.

From Forest Grove, head south on State 47 about 6 miles and turn right on Scoggins Valley Road. Drive 3.7 miles to the dam; continue another mile and turn left at the sign to the Recreation Area "A" West boat ramp. Scoggins Valley Park, surrounding the lake, closes in winter, opening just in time for fishing season. If the park is closed, park along the road and walk 0.2 mile down to the boat ramp.

The trail begins at the north end of the large boat-ramp parking area. It begins as a gravel path, leading quickly to a little viewing platform, then turns to dirt, where most casual strollers turn around. Cross several footbridges in the next mile as the trail curves through the forest following the reservoir's contours; trillium can be seen blooming in late March and early April.

The forest is lush here, with large cedars forming an airy canopy overhead. Pass a picnic table at a scenic spot; then, at 1.5 miles, pass another picnic table where the trail reaches the end of one long lake finger. Continue along the finger's shore, emerging from the woods at 2 miles onto a wide, open, grassy slope with a lovely, lapping beach, ideal for a leisurely lunch and some water play. Turn around here, or continue on for a longer hike.

72. Silver Creek Canyon: South Falls Loop

Type: Dayhike
Difficulty: Moderate
Distance: 5 miles, loop
Hikable: Year-round
Use: Heavy
High point: 1460 feet
Elevation gain: 360 feet
Maps: USGS Drake Crossing;
Silver Falls State Park
Trail Guide

Silver Falls State Park is one of Oregon's premier family parks, with hiking trails, paved bicycle paths, equestrian trails, and a great campground, all in a magnificent forested canyon with ten major waterfalls—and less than a half-hour from I-5. The configuration of trails offers numerous options, from short falls-viewing jaunts to longer loops.

Most popular is a 5-mile loop originating at South Falls that leads past, and in some cases behind, seven of the ten falls. Hikes here never seem long; there are always some surprises waiting around the corner. The canyon is appealing in all seasons, even winter, when subfreezing temperatures nearly freeze the falls in place. But mist from the falls coats the trails with ice, too, making hiking hazardous; it's wise to wait for warmer weather.

From I-5 near Salem, take exit 253 and follow State 22 southeast 5 miles to State 214; take it east 16.5 miles, following signs to the park, and turn left into South Falls Day Use Area. Follow signs to Picnic Area C and park at the far end of the lot. Follow the paved path past the restrooms a short distance to a low stone wall overlooking South Falls.

From there, take the paved path to the base of the falls; turn left at the junction to walk behind the falls. Follow the path past the footbridge below the falls. Cross it for a short loop back to the parking lot; otherwise, continue down the creek's left bank on the now unpaved (and often rocky and muddy) trail.

In 0.7 mile, Lower South Falls can be seen just before the trail plunges down 187 steps and winds behind the falls. The trail follows the south fork of Silver Creek downstream, veers away from the creek, then – what happened? The stream's flowing backward! Not really; the trail has passed the confluence and is now heading up the creek's north fork.

Upper North Falls

Just past Lower North Falls, take the short spur up Hult Creek to see tall, skinny Double Falls. At Middle North Falls, a spur leads behind the falls, but it's narrow, rough, and very slick and best avoided with kids.

To complete the loop, turn right over the footbridge 0.2 mile past Middle North Falls and follow a dainty side creek to the base of Winter Falls. Continue to the top of the falls, emerging at a small highway turnout. The trail resumes on the far side of the turnout, staying parallel to the road for about 0.5 mile (and converging briefly with a bicycle path a couple of times) before heading off into lovely old-growth forest.

When the trail meets the road, cross the road, pick up the trail again, and continue a short distance to a parking lot. Cross it, then follow a paved service road to the park's lodge. Walk past the lodge, then past the restrooms, and arrive back at the hike's start.

Older children ready for a challenge could combine this loop with Hike 73, the North Falls Loop, to create a 7-mile hike.

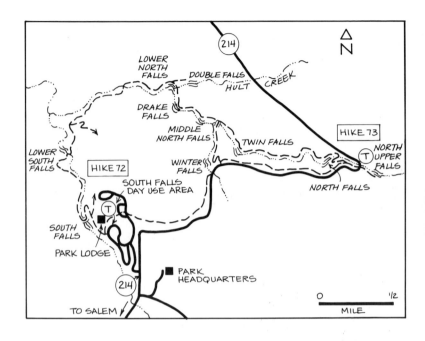

73. Silver Creek Canyon: North Falls Loop

Type:	Dayhike
Difficulty:	Easy
Distance:	3 miles, loop
Hikable:	Year-round
Use:	Heavy
High point:	1540 feet
Elevation gain:	220 feet
Maps:	USGS Drake Crossing and Elk Prairie; Silver Falls State Park Trail Guide

This hike is a shorter alternative to the more popular South Falls Loop (Hike 72). It leads over two footbridges and past three waterfalls, including the author's personal favorite, North Falls. The hike can be lengthened by continuing down the North Fork to see a few more falls, or shortened by turning around at Twin Falls.

For road directions to Silver Falls State Park, see Hike 72, South Falls Loop. From the turn-off to South Falls Day Use Area, continue on the main road another 2.3 miles and turn left into the North Falls trailhead parking area.

Cross the arching footbridge, bear left where a spur splits off to the right back under the bridge, then bear right at the next fork. In a few minutes the trail reaches the top of North Falls. Continue along the railed, cliff-hugging trail, then down seventy-eight steps and back behind the falls in a wide, deep, dry cave. The sound of the falls pounding the rocks below reverberates in the cave, sounding like a 747 at take-off. Walk with care; seeping water makes the trail slick in places.

Winter Falls

Continue downstream about 1 mile to Twin Falls, passing a huge split boulder resting in the creek. Past Twin Falls, turn left across the North Fork on a footbridge and follow a side creek up to Winter Falls. At the top of the falls, the trail reaches a highway turnout; the trail resumes on the left, following close to the road 1 mile back to the arching footbridge at the hike's start. Return to your car, or walk under the footbridge (and road bridge) and take a side trail another 0.2 mile upstream to see Upper North Falls. Return as you came.

74. Marys Peak Summit

Type:	Dayhike
Difficulty:	Easy
Distance:	1.4 miles round-trip
Hikable:	April through November
Use:	Heavy
High point:	4097 feet
Elevation gain:	337 feet
Maps:	USGS Marys Peak;
	Siuslaw National Forest

For an adult, the 0.7-mile walk up the gravel road leading to the tiptop of Marys Peak is pretty tame. To a young child new to hiking, it's an adventure. As the highest peak in the Coast Range, Marys Peak can feel like the top of the world to a youngster whose world isn't yet too big. Summer is the best season here, with penstemon, Columbia lilies, lupine, and other wildflowers festooning the upper slopes, but think of Marys Peak in shoulder seasons as well, when clouds sometimes swirl eerily around the treeless summit.

From U.S. 20 in Philomath, west of Corvallis, turn south onto Highway 34 and drive 9 miles to Marys Peak Road; turn right. Drive 10 miles to the summit parking lot.

The trail is really a gravel road, barred to all but utility vehicles servicing the transmission towers on the summit. From the parking area, the route is mostly above treeline, though you'll pass through stands of Douglas fir and noble fir; can the kids tell the difference? Suggest they look for cones at the base of the trees, to give them a hint.

Though relatively low by Cascades standards, Marys Peak is the highest point for thousands of miles from the west, and for more than 50 miles from the east; consequently, it can be windy on top. No place on a mountain

Trail up Marys Peak, shrouded in clouds

summit is really sheltered, but wander around to find the least windy side for a picnic.

When the kids are ready to graduate beyond this easy hike, consider lengthening it by linking it with the North Ridge or East Ridge Trail, both of which wind through the deep forest below the parking lot; get a trail guide at the Siuslaw National Forest office in Corvallis.

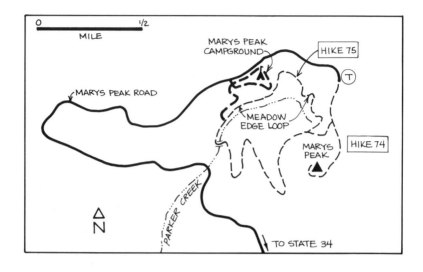

75. Meadow Edge Loop

Type:	Dayhike
Difficulty:	Easy
Distance:	1.9 miles, loop
Hikable:	April through November
Use:	Light
High point:	3880 feet
Elevation gain:	480 feet
Maps:	USGS Marys Peak;
	Siuslaw National Forest

In contrast to the simplicity of the Marys Peak summit hike, this loop trail is full of variety and fun. Just about any child can hike the trail, and the variety of habitats it traverses makes it clear the trail was constructed with young hikers in mind. The Meadow Edge Trail can be accessed via a spur leading off the Marys Peak summit trail or from a spur off the picnic area loop at Marys Peak Campground, 0.8 mile back down Marys Peak Road from the summit parking lot.

For road directions, see Marys Peak Summit (Hike 74).

From the summit trail, look for a signpost on the right about 0.2 mile from the parking lot trailhead. Walk the narrow path through the grassy meadow about 30 yards and enter a deep forest, where there is a trailhead sign and map. To walk the 1.5-mile loop clockwise, go straight at the first trail junction. Peek through the trees to see that the trail lies just inside the forest's edge. After a few minutes the trail emerges from the forest into a wildflower-strewn meadow, then loops back into the woods, which have their own summer carpet of bleeding hearts and oxalis.

Wind down through the airy old-growth forest to a little bridge crossing Parker Creek at about 0.8 mile. A short distance beyond the bridge

Crossing Parker Creek on Meadow Edge Trail

there's a spur leading left to Marys Peak Campground. To continue on the loop, bear right, walking uphill now. Notice that the trail once again lies right on the meadow's edge, just inside the forest. Continue along the forest's edge until reaching the start of the loop, bearing left to return to the summit trail.

76. Woodpecker Loop

Type:	Dayhike
Difficulty:	Easy
Distance:	1.2 miles, loop
Hikable:	Year-round
Use:	Light
High point:	420 feet
Elevation gain:	300 feet
Maps:	USGS Greenberry; Willamette Valley National Wildlife Refuges brochure

William L. Finley National Wildlife Refuge is one in a chain of three Willamette Valley refuges designated to provide winter habitat for several subspecies of Canada geese, including the dusky, whose numbers have been dwindling. The best time to visit the refuge is October through March, when there are sure to be plenty of geese. This loop trail winds through a variety of habitats typical of this transition zone between the Coast Range and the Willamette Valley; plan to wander it slowly, savoring all the opportunities for exploration (but watching for poison oak off-trail). It's the only trail in the refuge that's open through the winter; the others close to avoid disturbing the geese.

From Corvallis, take U.S. 99W south 10 miles and turn west at the sign to Finley refuge. After 1.3 miles, turn south and drive 2.3 miles to the signed trailhead for Woodpecker Loop, passing restrooms and a display kiosk at 0.8 mile.

Follow the trail past a signboard and pond, where the frog- and newt-catchers in the party can have a field day. Just 0.1 mile from the trailhead, the trail splits to start the loop. Bearing right, the trail reaches a huge oak encircled by a wooden platform at 0.3 mile; it looks out over a dry, grassy hillside scattered with more native oaks. Interpretive signs offer information about the area's ecology.

Continuing on, the nearly level trail winds mostly through a mixed

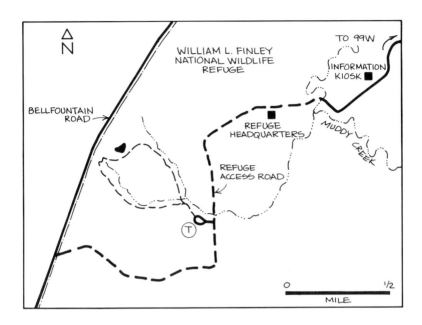

forest of big-leaf maple, Douglas fir, and Oregon white oak, dipping also into ash swales and dense stands of second-growth Douglas fir. Listen and look for woodpeckers along the way; five different kinds live along this trail.

Viewing platform circling oak on Woodpecker Loop

77. Mount Pisgah

Type: Dayhike
Difficulty: Moderate
Distance: 3 miles round-trip
Hikable: Year-round
Use: Heavy
High point: 1520 feet
Elevation gain: 1000 feet
Map: USGS Springfield

The way is steep and muddy in places, and hikers may have to pick their way through a minefield of "cow pies" in some sections. Nevertheless, the trail up Mount Pisgah, just minutes from Eugene, is well worth the effort, and not only for its views of the southern Willamette Valley and the mountains beyond. A bronze sighting pedestal installed at the summit in 1990 draws hikers of all ages; adults and kids are fascinated by its relief map of the area and the collage of leaves and seeds, shells, animals, birds, fish, and other life forms that have dwelt in Oregon over the past 200 million years, depicted in bas-relief on the pedestal's sides. Be sure to carry paper—lots of it—and crayons or pastels so that the kids can make rubbings of their favorite critters.

From Eugene or Springfield, take I-5 south to the Lane Community College/30th Avenue E. exit and follow signs about 2.5 miles, picking up Seavey Loop Road, to the arboretum. There's a trailhead just past the bridge over the Coast Fork of the Willamette River, but bear right and drive to the end of the parking lot at the arboretum instead. The trailhead here leads to a more gradual, less muddy route up the mountain.

Making rubbings on sighting pedestal atop Mount Pisgah

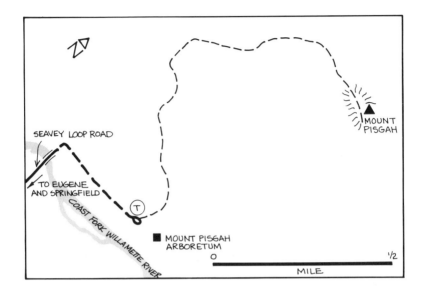

SEAVEY LOOP ROAD

TO EUGENE AND SPRINGFIELD

COAST FORK WILLAMETTE RIVER

MOUNT PISGAH

MOUNT PISGAH ARBORETUM

0   ½

MILE

From the trailhead, wind up through grassy meadows and in and out of oak groves, watching also for poison oak. You may stumble across a herd of cows, as Lane County leases much of the park for grazing; children will have fun mooing in passing. While ascending, enjoy the view to the west of the Coast Fork and across the lower Willamette Valley to Spencer Butte. Look for grasshoppers along the trail.

Unlike many view hikes, the trail grows more gradual as it ascends. At 1.5 miles, it emerges from a grove of oaks onto the grassy, treeless summit. The 40-inch-high pedestal is straight ahead. Before the kids get too engrossed in their rubbings (or after they've finished), show them how to use the relief map on top to identify local land forms: looking across the top, line up the map's Mount Pisgah (in the center of the map) with a real-life mountain or river seen from the summit, then locate that place on the map to identify it. Older children will be interested to know that the life forms depicted on the pedestal are arranged chronologically, with life forms from the middle Eocene (200 million years ago) on the bottom and contemporary life forms on top. Also notice the four world maps illustrating continental drift.

The pedestal is a memorial to two University of Oregon wrestlers, Jed Kesey and Lorenzo West, who were killed in an accident in the team van in 1984. Jed's parents, author Ken Kesey and his wife, Faye, commissioned the sculpture; their family farm is at the mountain's base.

Mount Pisgah Arboretum, at the base of the mountain, offers lots of opportunities for lowland hikes with young children, especially in spring, when wildflowers are blooming. The drive to Mount Pisgah, past small farms, is itself a treat for kids in most seasons: in summer there are you-pick berries, and in fall, pumpkins.

North Coast

U.S. 101, Columbia River to Newport

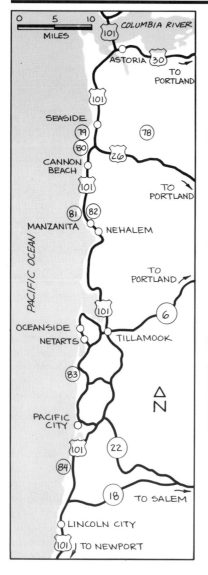

Stormy day at Ecola State Park

78. Saddle Mountain

Type: Dayhike
Difficulty: Difficult
Distance: 5.5 miles round-trip
Hikable: March through December
Use: Light
High point: 3283 feet
Elevation gain: 1600 feet
Maps: USGS Saddle Mountain;
Saddle Mountain State Park
Summit Trail Map

This hike, on the way from Portland to Seaside and Cannon Beach, is especially rewarding on clear days, when the view from the top stretches from Mount Rainier to the Pacific. The way is steep and rough in places (signs at the trailhead warn off all but the most experienced hikers), but the well-worn path is testimony to its popularity among all ages, and reconstruction scheduled for completion in 1992 should improve the trail's

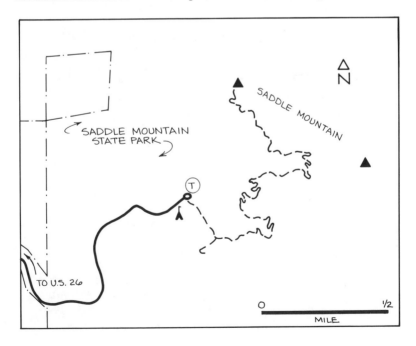

Saddle Mountain

condition. Children ready for the challenge of this climb will enjoy distinguishing—and reaching—the distinctly saddle-shaped summit ridge. May and June are especially good months for this hike, when a profusion of wildflowers—some of them unique to this area—are in bloom, though trail use at this time is heavy.

 From U.S. 26 (about 20 miles east of U.S. 101, and about 18 miles east of the Jewell junction), turn north at the sign for Saddle Mountain State Park. Continue about 7 miles to the end of the road and the small parking area at the trailhead.

The trail begins as an asphalt path, quickly narrowing to a forest footpath through alder and second-growth Douglas fir. At 0.2 mile, a spur to the right leads about 0.2 mile onto a rocky outcrop with a wonderful view of the mountain. Watch children carefully; the final scramble is difficult, even with cable railing in places.

Continuing on the main trail, break out of the forest about 1 mile from the trailhead. The next mile switchbacks up an open slope, strewn with wildflowers in late spring. While climbing, look back to see the rumpled patchwork of greens and browns stretching below, evidence of extensive clearcutting in the Coast Range.

The trail peaks at the saddle ridge, but you're not at the top yet. If the horse is headed north, you're about where the rider's tailbone would be and headed toward the pommel.

Follow the trail as it slides down the ridge and climbs back up to the summit at the saddle's north end. Kids can play detective, looking for clues of the fire lookout that once stood here. In the meantime, enjoy the view of Mount Rainier, Mount Hood, Mount St. Helens, and Mount Adams—if skies permit—plus Astoria and the Pacific.

After the hike, if headed to the coast, drop by Fort Clatsop National Memorial just south of Astoria. Here youngsters can explore the reconstructed fort where Lewis and Clark and company spent the winter of 1805–06. Looking south, they can see Saddle Mountain towering above the surrounding Coast Range peaks, for a different perspective on their achievement.

79. Tillamook Head

Type:	Dayhike or backpack
Difficulty:	Moderate to difficult
Distance:	6 miles one way
Hikable:	Year-round
Use:	Light
High point:	1150 feet
Elevation gain:	900 feet
Map:	USGS Tillamook Head

The fun here is the challenge of walking from Seaside almost to Cannon Beach, more fun if the kids are familiar with both towns. Highway engineers went out of their way to avoid Tillamook Head when they laid out U.S. 101. On foot, hikers can be bolder. A round-trip hike can be made from either end, with Clarks Viewpoint or the ruins of a World War II gun battery near the tip of the head as the destination. It's even fun to hike in the winter; the deep woods provide some shelter from rain. Be sure to wear waterproof boots and rain pants, as the trail gets mighty

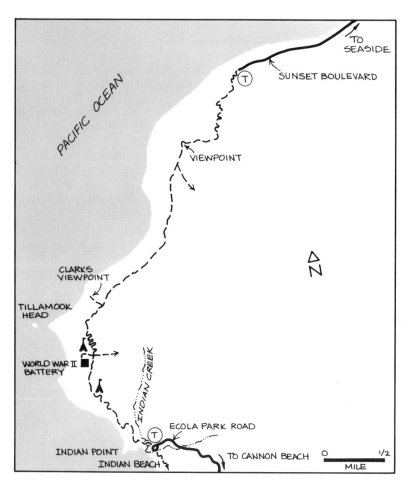

muddy and the trailside vegetation awfully drippy.

To reach the northern trailhead from the Seaside junction of U.S. 26 and 101, take U.S. 101 north 2.7 miles and turn left at the first signal, on Avenue U. Drive 0.2 mile, turn left onto South Edgewood Road, and continue 1.2 miles as it becomes Sunset Boulevard, passing a golf course, to the end of the road. As an alternative, start the hike on the beach in Seaside, walking south until reaching a scramble trail that leads up Tillamook Head to the golf course road (for road directions to the southern trailhead at Indian Point, see Hike 80, Indian Point—Ecola Point.)

From the northern trailhead, pick up the trail at the southeast end of the parking area. The toughest part of the hike is the first 1.5 miles, as the trail switchbacks up about 700 feet onto Tillamook Head. At 1 mile there's a good view to the north of Seaside and, beyond it, Cape Disappointment across the Columbia River. Continue another 0.5 mile, bearing right at a junction, where the trail levels out.

Roll along through deep forest to 3.7 miles, where a plaque announces Clarks Viewpoint. That's Clark of Lewis and Clark; during their famous expedition they wintered at a fort (Fort Clatsop) they built near Astoria and traveled to Seaside on virtually this same route.

From the viewpoint, the trail drops a bit, then reaches a campsite with an outhouse at an old road crossing at 4.4 miles. Follow the road west 0.2 mile to see the old artillery battery, nearly obscured by vegetation; it was built as part of a series of coastal defense fortifications during World War II. Near the outhouse, look for a huge stump with springboard notches cut by early-day loggers.

The trail leads uphill a bit, then levels out and starts dropping. Look around the forest here for nurse logs and for big stumps, left over from old logging operations. At 4.8 miles the trail passes a small, level clearing that would make a nice campsite. Then it drops down along Indian Creek, crosses it on a footbridge, and ends at Indian Beach.

Springboard notches on Tillamook Head stump

80. Indian Point–Ecola Point

Type:	Dayhike
Difficulty:	Easy
Distance:	1.5 miles one way
Hikable:	Year-round
Use:	Light
High point:	150 feet
Elevation gain:	100 feet
Map:	USGS Tillamook Head

The path between Ecola and Indian points leads above a rocky and dramatic stretch of coastline inaccessible to all but hikers. It's a fun, easy hike for families vacationing in Cannon Beach. In winter, mudslides often close the park road between the two points for long stretches. At those times, make a loop hike from Ecola Point, returning via the road. (Don't do it if the road is open, however; it's narrow, and there's no shoulder for pedestrians.) Hike the trail north to south in summer, to keep the wind at your back. It's even fun during a winter storm, since the woods offer significant protection; just reverse your direction to keep the sou'wester from spattering your face.

From the Seaside junction of U.S. 26 and 101, take U.S. 101 south

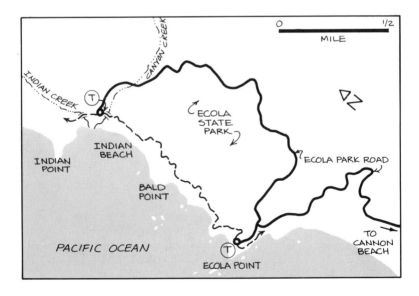

Looking south from Indian Point

3 miles and take the first Cannon Beach exit. Follow the road down the hill and turn right at the sign to Ecola State Park. (From "downtown" Cannon Beach, follow Hemlock Street north until across Ecola Creek and turn left to the park.) Follow signs 2 miles to the southern trailhead parking area at Ecola Point (if using a shuttle car, leave it here), then continue another 1.7 miles to Indian Beach to make the hike north to south (with the wind at your back).

From the Indian Beach parking lot, follow the sign to the ocean beach. Cross the creek, then bear left at the fork, rather than right to the beach. The trail alternates between woodsy path and shoreline vista trail as it rolls along 100 to 150 feet over the ocean. At about 0.5 mile, the trail reaches a rather steep slide area. At 0.8 mile, the trail crosses an open slope with flowers in the spring, a good spot to rest and watch for fishing boats in summer. The trail emerges from the woods at the edge of the Ecola Point parking area at 2 miles.

81. Cape Falcon

Type:	Dayhike
Difficulty:	Moderate
Distance:	5 miles round-trip
Hikable:	Year-round
Use:	Light
High point:	240 feet
Elevation gain:	300 feet
Map:	USGS Arch Cape

The hike out to Cape Falcon leads through a wonderful coastal forest with all its delights: birds twittering, shafts of sunlight playing through the lacy conifer branches, and trickling creeks. At the end, follow a narrow

Cream-colored fungus on mossy log

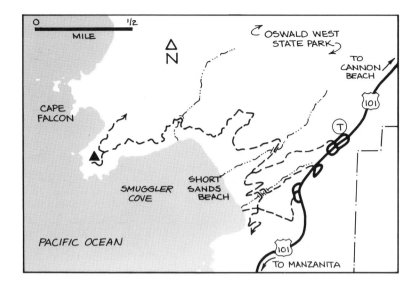

corridor onto the grassy, brushy, but treeless cape, where children will have fun following mazes in the salal and watching for fishing boats offshore.

From Cannon Beach, take U.S. 101 south 10 miles and turn right into the first west-side parking area for Oswald West State Park.

A maze of loop trails winds through the forest here; for the simplest approach to Cape Falcon, take the trail that leaves the north end of the first parking area on the west side of the highway. The trail winds through an inspiring forest above Short Sands Creek, roaring to its meeting with the Pacific. At about 0.5 mile, turn right at the trail junction. (A left turn leads a short distance to Short Sands Beach; drop in on the way back.) Soon the trail crosses a small creek and, at 1 mile, enters an old logged-off blowdown area. Immediately past it, see the kinds of trees that had blown down: huge spruce, hemlock, and Douglas fir.

The trail continues to roll along, crossing small creeks. On a sunny day the ocean can be seen sparkling through the trees. At about 1.8 miles, the trail enters a clearing, granting views south to Short Sands Beach and Neahkahnie Mountain. At 2 miles, after a climb up a couple of short switchbacks, there's an even better view. Continue following the contours of the hill on the mostly level path to a junction, unsigned, with a spur trail leading west out onto the top of Cape Falcon. Follow it 0.2 mile, through a virtual tunnel of salal at first, onto the treeless, wind-swept cape tip, a dramatic spot. It's not particularly hazardous as long as children use reasonable care, but the cliffs are steep. The trail, part of the long-distance Oregon Coast Trail, continues north toward Arch Cape; to return to the parking area, retrace your steps.

82. Neahkahnie Mountain

Type: Dayhike
Difficulty: Moderate
Distance: 3 miles round-trip
Hikable: Year-round
Use: Heavy
High point: 1631 feet
Elevation gain: 890 feet
Map: USGS Nehalem

Legend has it that somewhere on Neahkahnie Mountain a 200-year-old treasure-trove lies buried, waiting to be discovered. Whether or not it's true, it's a great source of speculation on a trek to the summit of this looming north coast landmark. The easiest way up is from the south, though a trail leads to the summit from the west as well.

From Manzanita, drive north on U.S. 101 for 1.5 miles to a hiker sign, turn east on a very rocky, slow-going access road, and continue 0.5 mile to the trailhead. There is room for several cars to park. Southbound, the access road is about 13 miles south of Cannon Beach.

The trail ascends steadily, switchbacking up the hillside in and out of gloomy Sitka spruce stands and open hillsides thick with salal and salmonberry or, in spring, such wildflowers as the sky-pink coast fawn lily. The fourth switchback (0.5 mile from the trailhead) offers the first of many great views. It's a view even a kid can love, with lots of recog-

nizable landmarks, including U.S. 101, the Nehalem River and Bay, and the towns of Nehalem and Wheeler.

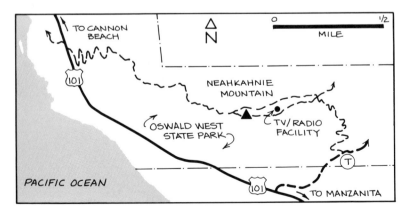

Sitka spruce tunnel on Neahkahnie Mountain trail

Continue up the mountain's south side, up more than a dozen switchbacks, to a wooden trail marker post at the summit ridge (1.2 miles). Bear left up the forest road to a collection of radio and TV antennas at a cement-block building. Round the building on a rough trail and continue a few steps through the woods to the tiny, knobby summit. It's a great perch for a picnic on a sunny day. Children must take care in climbing around, as the hillside is steep.

With children, it's best to return as you came. It's also possible to hike a loop route, returning to the summit ridge and continuing around the back of the mountain and down its west face. Then there's more than a mile of walking along busy U.S. 101, some of it (but not all) on a footpath parallel to the highway.

83. Cape Lookout

Type:	Dayhike
Difficulty:	Moderate
Distance:	5 miles round-trip
Hikable:	Year-round
Use:	Heavy
High point:	850 feet
Elevation gain:	400 feet
Map:	USGS Sand Lake

The great appeal of a hike to the tip of Cape Lookout is the chance to spot whales—motivation enough for some children. Cape Lookout is considered the best whale-watching site on the Oregon coast, and with more than two hundred gray whales now summering off Oregon, the chances of spotting a whale in midsummer aren't bad. Unfortunately, the best times are when the trail is at its muddiest: mid-March, during the northward migration, and December through early January, when the migrants

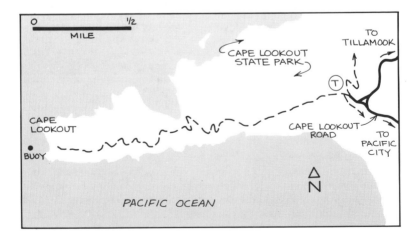

Windfall area on Cape Lookout trail

are headed to south Baja for the winter. At those times, an average of fifteen to thirty whales may pass by in a hour. Trail use, however, is light in winter.

Even if whales aren't sighted, the hike itself is worthwhile. Take it slow and easy, enjoying the views and the forest along the way. After the hike, drive south to Pacific City and look north at the long headland sticking way out from the mainland to see what you just accomplished.

From Tillamook, follow signs west and south about 10 miles to the entrance to Cape Lookout State Park and campground. Rather than turning here, however, continue another 2.8 miles on Cape Lookout Road to a trailhead parking area on the right. From Pacific City, follow Three Capes Scenic Route north about 13 miles to the trailhead.

Two trails start side by side at the west end of the parking area. The trail on the right leads north on a woodsy, up-and-down route 2.5 miles to the park's campground. Instead, take the lefthand trail. In about 75 yards, go straight where another trail comes in from the left (it leads 2 miles down to the beach).

The terrain that the trail follows to the cape tip is rolling, but mostly slowly descending. At 0.6 mile the forest opens up to grand views of the beach and headlands to the south. From here, kids can watch on the right for a plaque memorializing the victims of a 1943 plane crash. At 1.2 miles—about the halfway point—the trail reaches a fenced cliff on the north side of the cape, granting views of Oceanside and Three Arch Rocks.

The route wends back to the cape's south side, teasing hikers on with occasional views. A single strand of wire cable strung along the cliff does little more than warn hikers to take care; children may not get the hint,

217

so watch them here. While approaching the tip, kids can listen for the buoy anchored offshore, moaning with the rhythm of the swells. Once they spot it, it's just a few more minutes' walk to the rocky point at the trail's end. Carry a picnic and binoculars and plan to linger awhile if hoping to spot any whales, as the whales travel on their own schedule.

84. Harts Cove

Type:	Dayhike or backpack
Difficulty:	Moderate to difficult
Distance:	5.8 miles round-trip
Hikable:	Year-round
Use:	Light
High point:	960 feet
Elevation gain:	800 feet
Map:	USGS Neskowin

The hike to Harts Cove is more like a mountain hike than a beach hike—think of it in those terms and you won't be disappointed. In fact, you'll probably be enchanted. The hike doesn't go up a high headland or down to a secluded beach, but leads to a grassy slope overlooking a particularly dramatic and remote stretch of coastline. On the way the trail winds through a magnificent hemlock and Sitka spruce forest and crosses a couple of rushing streams on footbridges. Most of the elevation loss (and on the return, gain) is in the first mile; after that, it's a pleasant stroll.

From Neskowin, take U.S. 101 south 3.6 miles and turn right on Cascade Head Road (Road 1861), which is 4 miles south of State 18. Follow Road 1861 for 4.1 miles to the trailhead at road's end and park.

The trail drops quickly, steeply at times, switchbacking down the hill until it reaches Cliff Creek at 1 mile. Cross the creek, its bank lush with wildflowers in the spring. From here the trail climbs gently; listen for the sounds of birds and the rush of the creek, slowly fading. At about 1.5 miles the crash of waves can be heard on the cliffs below; from October through May, the loud barking of California sea lions can be heard as well.

Shortly a sign announces the Neskowin Crest Research Area and suggests looking around at the remains of 250-year-old Sitka spruce that have survived fires that destroyed other trees in the forest. Just beyond the sign is a bench offering the first view of Harts Cove. It looks so close —but it's a good mile away by trail. Follow the trail back up a ravine,

Footbridge across Cliff Creek

across Chitwood Creek, then back through the loveliest, quietest, most magnificent old-growth forest yet seen along the trail. At 2.7 miles the trail emerges from the forest near the top of the grassy slope that overlooks Harts Cove to the south. Walk down the slope another 0.2 mile to peek down at the cove. There's lots of room to play and explore without getting too close to the cliffs, but adults will want to watch children carefully just the same. In case there's any doubt, assure members of your party that there is no safe way to climb down to the beach at Harts Cove.

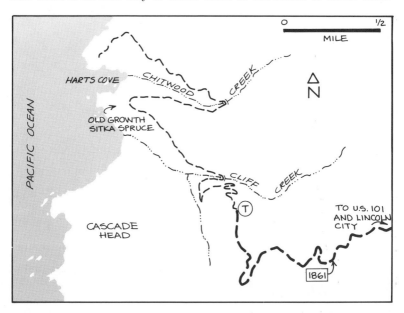

Central Coast

U.S. 101, Newport to Florence

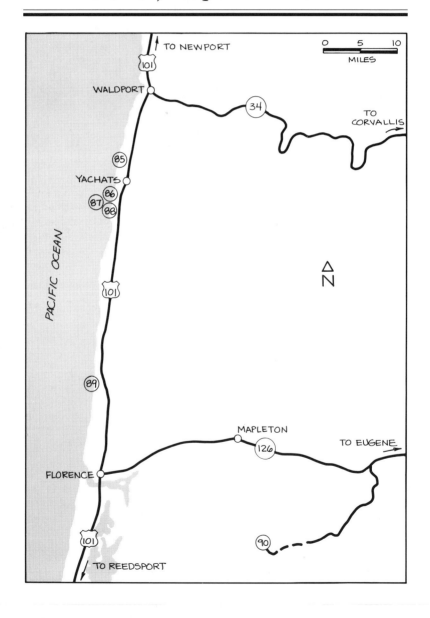

85. Yachats 804 Trail

Type: Dayhike
Difficulty: Easy
Distance: 1.7 miles round-trip
Hikable: Year-round
Use: Heavy
High point: 10 feet
Elevation gain: Negligible
Map: USGS Yachats

The 804 Trail is an old road that's been reclaimed for pedestrians as part of the Oregon Coast Trail. It runs between private homes and the beach at first, then leads to a more remote stretch of coast. Its main attraction is a fascinating stretch of wave-sculpted rocks and even a blowhole that kids will find irresistible.

From "downtown" Yachats, drive north 0.5 mile and turn west at the sign to Smelt Sands Wayside. The gravel road leads 0.3 mile to a parking area and signed trailhead.

Just past the trailhead there are picnic tables perched on the bluff and a small, sandy beach below—something to return to at the end of the hike? The wide, compacted-gravel path, which is partially paved for wheelchair accessibility, veers north, following right along the edge of the bluff overlooking a shelf of fantastically shaped rocks. A few steps down the trail there's a rock tunnel that becomes a wild blowhole at or near high tide. Children must take some care with their footing while scrambling over the rocks.

The trail continues along the bluff, passing a few private homes and

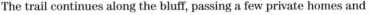

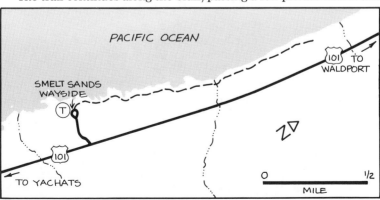

Sea-sculpted rocks along Yachats 804 Trail

a motel and gradually growing more isolated. Cross a little sandy chasm, then continue north, hugging the bluff's edge, to reach a wonderful shelf of smooth boulders at about 0.7 mile. Kids can spend hours playing on the rock shelf; if weather permits, find a depression and soak up some sun out of the wind. Just beyond the rocks is a beach signifying the end of the trail.

86. Cape Perpetua Summit

Type:	Dayhike
Difficulty:	Moderate
Distance:	3 miles round-trip
Hikable:	Year-round
Use:	Light
High point:	746 feet
Elevation gain:	640 feet
Maps:	USGS Yachats;
	Siuslaw National Forest

It's possible to drive to the top of Cape Perpetua as well as walk there, but why not walk? There's a lot of SPM (satisfaction per mile) walking from nearly sea level to 746 feet, watching the coastline unfurl below you. With enough adults in the party, an alternative is to drive up, then have a driver meet the rest of the party at the bottom after they've walked down. The group may even beat the driver back to the trailhead, and it's a shoo-in they'll have more fun.

From Yachats, drive south 2.5 miles and turn left at the sign to Cape Perpetua Scenic Area visitor center. The gates close at 5:00 P.M. in summer

Rock shelter atop Cape Perpetua

and earlier in winter; if you expect to be out hiking after closing, park along the highway and walk the short distance to the visitor center.

Excellent signs at the visitor center include detailed maps of this and other trails around Cape Perpetua. Begin hiking just east of the center and head down an asphalt path bordered by dense walls of salal and salmonberry. Cross Cape Creek on a plank footbridge and follow the trail across the campground road and, at 0.4 mile, across the auto-tour road.

St. Perpetua Trail begins across the road, starting out pretty steep as it switchbacks up the south side of the cape, but mellowing soon. At about 0.7 mile the route leads up some stone steps through a clearing cut for power lines. Most of the way the spruce-and-alder woods are too dense to allow anything more than peekaboo views, but at about 1.3 miles, the trail emerges from the trees to get an almost dizzying view of the coast to the south (barring fog). The terrain stays mostly open and grassy as the trail switchbacks to the top.

Extend the hike 0.3 mile, if desired, with a walk along the partially paved Whispering Spruce summit loop. The high point is a rock shelter built in 1933 by the Civilian Conservation Corps. The Coast Guard used it during World War II to look for enemy ships; the kids will have fun trying to spot whales.

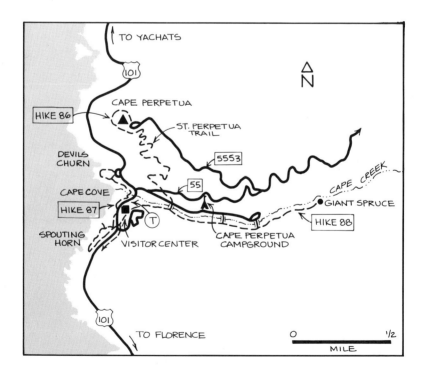

87. Cape Perpetua Shoreline Loop

Type:	Dayhike
Difficulty:	Easy
Distance:	1.3 miles, loop
Hikable:	Year-round
Use:	Heavy
High point:	140 feet
Elevation gain:	200 feet
Maps:	USGS Yachats;
	Siuslaw National Forest

There are lots of places to tidepool along the Oregon coast, many not requiring any hiking at all. With this tidepool hike, getting there is half the fun. The trail passes under the highway in a huge culvert, crosses footbridges, and descends wooden stairs to get to a series of natural attractions at the base of Cape Perpetua. If the tide is out, there are tidepools to explore; if it happens to be in, the blowholes in the rocks become the main attraction. In fact, children won't even know they're on a hike unless it's called that.

From the Cape Perpetua Scenic Area visitor center (see Hike 86, Cape Perpetua Summit), follow signs down a trail heading west, under the highway. At the end of the tunnel, turn left toward Spouting Horn (a right turn leads north to Devils Churn). Turn left again, walk through a tree tunnel, then down steps to see Spouting Horn, a hole in the top of a sea cave that spouts air and water when incoming waves build pressure inside the cave. Continue around to the north to do some tidepooling, if tides permit.

Between the tidepools and the culvert, notice the mounds on the bluff above the beach. They're Indian middens—essentially garbage dumps—used by the Alsi Indians between about A.D. 600 and 1620. Archeologists believe the Alsi camped here in the summer while collecting mussels and other shellfish to eat. They tossed the discarded shells in a heap, along with bones from fish, birds, and animals they caught.

When ready to continue the loop, follow the trail up to the parking area along the highway at 0.6 mile, then walk along the highway (inside the guardrail) a short distance to where the footpath resumes, leading down toward Cape Cove. A spur to the left leads to Cape Cove Beach; the main trail continues around the head of the cove, crosses the creek (on top of a well-buried culvert), and curves around to meet a trail junction signaling the start of 0.3-mile Devils Churn Loop.

Tidepooling below Cape Perpetua

Bear left, along the shore, to where stairs zigzag down to Devils Churn, a dead-end rock chute where waves race in and crash dramatically, drenching too-close visitors. It was formed over thousands of years through the sometimes patient process of erosion; a crack in the basalt slab at the sea's edge was slowly worn into the chute seen today by the pounding of zillions of waves.

To complete the loop, follow the trail up to the Devils Churn parking area and back down to the trail junction north of Cape Cove, then head south. For a quicker return from Devils Churn, just retrace your route.

88. Giant Spruce

Type: Dayhike
Difficulty: Easy
Distance: 2 miles round-trip
Hikable: Year-round
Use: Heavy
High point: 200 feet
Elevation gain: 140 feet
Maps: USGS Yachats;
Siuslaw National Forest

The destination on this short, level hike is a 500-year-old Sitka spruce that kids can crawl under, thanks apparently to its having sprouted on a nurse log that's long since decayed and disappeared. The hike is ideal for preschoolers, or for anyone looking for a short, leg-stretching outing along the coast. The trail follows Cape Creek closely most of the way to the giant spruce, providing musical accompaniment along the walk.

Footbridge along Giant Spruce Trail

From the Cape Perpetua Scenic Area visitor center (see Hike 86, Cape Perpetua Summit), follow the paved path that begins just east of the visitor center, and head down toward Cape Creek. The path reaches a footbridge at 0.2 mile, but rather than crossing the creek into the campground, continue along its south bank on the now-dirt path another 0.6 mile to a footbridge at the end of the campground. (An alternative is to drive to this point and start here, for a really short hike.)

From this point, it's just 0.2 mile to the giant spruce, most of it level with one stretch of climbing. The famed tree is about 15 feet in diameter and was 225 feet tall—until a 1962 windstorm snapped off its upper 35 feet.

89. China Creek–Hobbit Loop

Type: Dayhike
Difficulty: Easy to moderate
Distance: 3 to 4 miles, loop
Hikable: Year-round
Use: Light
High point: 200 feet
Elevation gain: 200 feet
Maps: USGS Heceta Head;
Carl G. Washburne
State Park brochure

What would a hobbit's trail look like? It would most likely be sort of hidden, like a little tunnel through deep woods, with fantastical, moss-covered trees. It might even be a little spooky, and it should lead someplace really special.

The 0.25-mile Hobbit Trail leading from U.S. 101 to the beach at Carl Washburne State Park fits that description to a T. It's not particularly well marked, but it's easy to find if you know where to look. Hike it as a round-trip walk to a remote stretch of beach, or link it with other trails in the park, passing by beaver ponds and through a grassy, open meadow, to make a 3- or 4-mile round-trip hike that includes a mile or more of beach walking. Another option is to make a one-way hike between the two highway trailheads, using a shuttle car.

If camping at Washburne, about 12 miles north of Florence off U.S. 101, pick up the trail where it passes through the camping loop (the park office should have trail brochures with a map). Otherwise, park at the

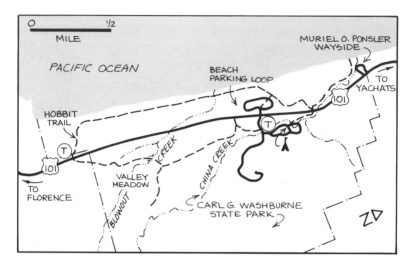

small trailhead turnout on the east side of U.S. 101 1.2 miles south of the entrance to Washburne State Park and 0.8 mile north of Devils Elbow State Park. Cars zoom by pretty fast on the highway here; watch kids carefully while lacing shoes and packing packs.

If interested in hiking just the Hobbit Trail to the beach, look for the wooden post marking the start of the trail across U.S. 101 from the trailhead parking area and a bit to the north. The path winds through a forest of pines and spruce and tall rhododendrons, twisting downhill 0.25 mile. It's easy to imagine running into a hobbit scurrying along this trail— or to imagine you are one yourself! Near the end, the trees close in briefly to create a tunnel. Then suddenly you're in a narrow chute lined with towering salal bushes for a few steps, then on the beach just north of massive Heceta Head.

To hike the whole loop, start in the opposite direction, following the trail on the east side of the highway as it leads north (this way, the north wind is at your back on the beach stretch). Drop down to an almost level path; children can watch on the right as a moist area turns into a black slough, then into a slow-moving stream. At 0.5 mile the trail reaches a couple of ponds hidden in the trees. Approach them quietly and you may see birds or even a beaver; you'll probably see plenty of evidence of beavers, in the form of fallen trees and stumps gnawed to a point.

The trail crosses Blowout Creek, then continues to a trail junction in a clearing in the middle of the forest at 1.3 miles; this is Valley Meadow. It can be refreshingly windless here on sunny summer days, and it's a nice spot for a picnic or just a pause. A spur trail leads east a short distance into the forest, for those who want more exploring. Otherwise, continue north up a hill and onto a lane walled with shore pines. Reach the paved campground access road at about 1.6 miles.

Entering Valley Meadow

To make a 3-mile loop, follow the trail west to the highway, across the highway to the beach parking loop, and pick up the trail through the loop. It emerges at the restrooms. Walk past the restrooms to the beach and start walking south on the sand. For a 4-mile loop, follow the paved campground road to the end of the campground and pick up the paved path heading north. It leads under the highway along China Creek and emerges near the creek at the beach. Turn south on a band of hard sand headed to Heceta Head, looming beyond.

Take your time heading down the beach; it's about 1.7 miles of walking from China Creek, 1.2 miles for shortcutters. When approaching the headland, look left into the foredune for a wooden post marking the start of the Hobbit Trail. Be careful at the trail's end, where it emerges from the forest across U.S. 101 from the south trailhead, as there's not much of a shoulder here.

90. Kentucky Falls

Type: Dayhike
Difficulty: Moderate
Distance: 4 miles round-trip
Hikable: Year-round
Use: Light
High point: 1560 feet
Elevation gain: 760 feet
Maps: USGS Baldy Mtn.;
Siuslaw National Forest

It's necessary to drive a bit to get to the trailhead for Kentucky Falls, but it's worth it. The hike in is easy—almost too easy; it's mostly downhill, and the trail ends at a pair of side-by-side waterfalls at the confluence of two creeks. Winter rains swell the falls, adding to their drama. Though the trail is snow-free virtually all year, snow sometimes blocks the road around 2862-foot Roman Nose mountain; in winter, call the Mapleton Ranger Station for road conditions.

From State 126 about 35 miles west of Eugene, or the same distance east of Florence, turn south at the sign to Clay Creek and Whittaker Creek Recreation Site. After 1.5 miles, turn right at the sign to Kentucky Falls Trail and continue following signs 14 miles (all but 4.5 miles are paved) to the signed trailhead off Road 919. You can also drive here from Reedsport, but it's a longer trip.

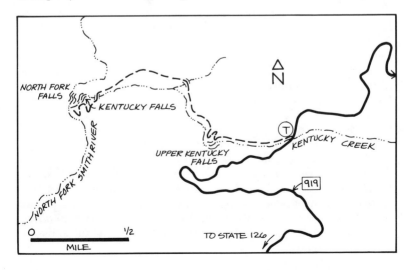

Kentucky Falls

Follow the trail into gorgeous old-growth and second-growth forest, listening for bird songs and looking for wildflowers in spring. After about 0.6 mile of fairly level walking, the trail reaches a viewpoint overlooking Upper Kentucky Falls. The trail then drops quickly to the falls' base.

The trail follows Kentucky Creek, then winds away from it a short distance to cross a side creek on a railed log bridge at 1.4 miles. For the last 0.4 mile the trail switchbacks steadily into the canyon, signaling to children that they're nearing the end (and that they'd better steel themselves for the return hike).

At the trail's end, both the North Fork Smith River and Kentucky Creek can be seen cascading down a cliff just upstream of the two creeks' confluence. A wooden viewing platform at the end covers a tangle of boulders that used to make viewing the falls a dangerous proposition for all but the most nimble-footed; now it's quite safe. Explore around the base of the falls a bit before turning around and tackling the return trip. The Forest Service plans to extend the trail another 5 miles down the North Fork Smith River.

South Coast

U.S. 101, Florence to Brookings

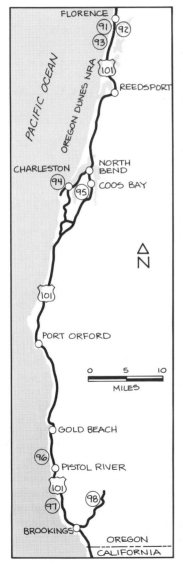

Oregon Dunes National Recreation Area

91. Waxmyrtle Trail

Type:	Dayhike
Difficulty:	Easy
Distance:	3 miles round-trip
Hikable:	Year-round
Use:	Light
High point:	40 feet
Elevation gain:	Negligible
Maps:	USGS Tahkenitch Creek; USFS Oregon Dunes National Recreation Area

This trail follows the meandering Siltcoos River for its last 1.5 miles before reaching the ocean. It's short enough for almost any child, and the ever-present opportunity to see wild birds on or near the river gives kids something to do as they walk. The changing topography also keeps things interesting. At the end, there's the beach—always a popular destination; be sure to pack in a kite!

 From Florence, drive south on U.S. 101 about 8 miles and turn west at the sign to Siltcoos Beach access. In about a mile, turn left into Waxmyrtle Campground, then immediately left again into the day-use parking area. The trail starts across the campground road at the signed trailhead.

Follow the path west along the south bank of the Siltcoos, first in dense dune shrubbery and then into a forest of shore pines. At about 0.3 mile, stairs of logs and sand lead up a short hill; at about 0.8 mile, the trail emerges from the forest into open, grassy dunes. Along the way, be watching the river for cormorants, kingfishers, great blue herons, and other water-loving birds.

After the trail opens up, it's about a 0.7-mile walk to the ocean heading west through the sandy dunes south of the river. For more wildlife-watching, climb on top of the tall foredune to the south; behind it is a marsh with more wildlife, including beaver and nutria. The marsh is an old channel of the Siltcoos that was cut off over time; now it's fed strictly by rainwater.

Back at the trailhead, the outing could be extended with a walk along the 0.5-mile River of No Return loop trail that follows another old arm of the Siltcoos River around Lagoon Campground, across the road from Waxmyrtle Campground. It begins as a boardwalk and turns into a foot-

Siltcoos River and Waxmyrtle Trail

path with bridges here and there across marshy spots. It can be noisy—
dune buggy enthusiasts like to camp here—but is still a worthwhile place
to do some nature-watching. Look carefully among the reeds at the water's
edge; what looks like a reed may actually be the reedlike beak of a
bittern, pointed to the sky and unmoving as it tries to go unnoticed.
Cinnamon teal, mallards, and Canada geese, as well as a number of
songbird species, nest here in summer; look for their chicks.

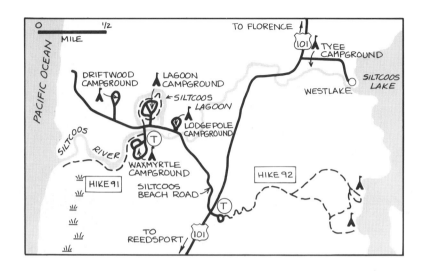

92. Siltcoos Lake

Type:	Dayhike or backpack
Difficulty:	Moderate
Distance:	4.4 miles round-trip
Hikable:	Year-round
Use:	Light
High point:	380 feet
Elevation gain:	600 feet
Maps:	USGS Tahkenitch Creek and Fivemile Creek; USFS Oregon Dunes National Recreation Area

Oregon Dunes National Recreation Area offers any number of hiking possibilities to families. What's special about this hike is the deep coastal forest it traverses, making it quite distinct from other trails in the area. At the end is a lake with campsites along the bank. (Boaters use the campsites, too.) The hike provides opportunities to explain changes in coastal logging practices over the past century, from springboard notches in huge stumps to trailside clearcuts.

The trailhead is just across U.S. 101 from the road to Siltcoos Beach access, about 8 miles south of Florence. From the trailhead, follow the

Trail to Siltcoos Lake

trail up a steady incline, starting along a corridor of dense salal and salmonberry some 10 feet tall. At about 0.7 mile the trail levels out and rolls along until forking at 1 mile. Either direction will lead to the lake in a little more than a mile.

Bearing left along the north route, the trail rises a bit, then starts dropping slowly through the second-growth forest. Look for springboard notches in a big cedar stump on the right side of the trail at about 1.3 miles. Watch ahead for the forest to start opening; that's Siltcoos Lake. At 2.2 miles the first of the lakeside campsites is reached, then a trail sign indicating the north and south routes back to U.S. 101. There's an outhouse ahead and more campsites.

When ready to return, get back on the trail and follow signs to U.S. 101 via the south route. In a few minutes the trail reaches a log boardwalk that snakes 25 yards to the base of a staircase heading uphill. A spur trail 0.7 mile from the lake leads south to more campsites. The trail skirts the edge of a clearcut at about 1 mile, then reaches the trail junction again 1.3 miles from the lake. Bear left to return to the trailhead parking area.

93. Oregon Dunes Overlook Loop

Type:	Dayhike
Difficulty:	Moderate to difficult
Distance:	3.3 miles, loop
Hikable:	Year-round
Use:	Light
High point:	140 feet
Elevation gain:	300 feet
Maps:	USGS Tahkenitch Creek; USFS Oregon Dunes National Recreation Area

The Oregon Dunes Overlook was built to give motorists a taste of the dunes on a quick detour off U.S. 101. It's also the trailhead for a wonderfully varied loop hike that takes in open dunes, the ocean beach, tree islands, and coastal forest. Though there's not much elevation gain, it's more difficult than comparable 3.3-mile forest hikes because much of the walking is on soft sand. Children will enjoy finding the route across the shifting dunes, where posts, not a permanent path, mark the way.

 From Reedsport, the overlook is about 10 miles north on U.S. 101. Signs direct hikers to the trail from either the upper viewing deck or the covered viewing structure off the parking lot. Walk the loop counterclockwise, to put the wind at your back on the beach.

Begin by crossing about 0.3 mile of open sand, watching for posts that

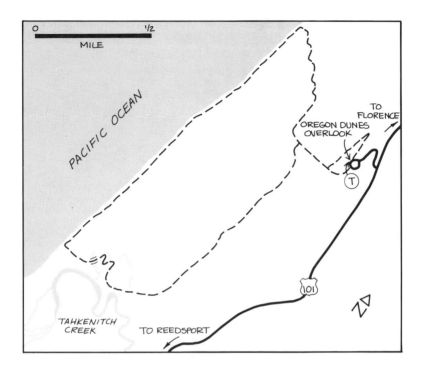

mark the route. Bear right with the loop trail as it winds into the deflation plain, a moist area just behind the foredune that's characterized by rushes, sedges, and other vegetation. Bridges keep feet dry through the wetter areas.

Climb up over the foredune and drop down onto the beach. Walk south along the shore, following the bands of harder sand to make walking easier. The trail through the dunes resumes in 1.5 miles; look for a post in the foredune marking the trail after about 30 minutes of steady walking at an easy adult pace, longer with young children. It's easy to spot if you're looking; if you hit Tahkenitch Creek, you've gone too far.

The trail leads up and over the foredune, granting a glimpse of Tahkenitch Creek on the right; pause to look for ospreys and bald eagles. Cross a little footbridge 0.2 mile from the beach, then shortly head up into a tall "island" of shore pines. From the summit the creek can be spotted again. Drop down the other side of the island and begin trekking across a Sahara-like landscape of open dunes, following marker posts leading to another tree island. Climb around its west side, then get back on the open sand. Skirt west of the next big tree island. (Look carefully for the post here; it's deeply buried in sand and hard to spot.) Just before reaching the end of the loop in the open sand below the overlook, the trail enters the deflation plain and becomes a narrow, sandy path.

Hiking post-to-post across the dunes

After, or preferably before, the hike, stop at the Oregon Dunes National Recreation Area headquarters, off U.S. 101 in Reedsport, for more information on the geology and ecology of the dunes, some of it geared to youngsters, as well as other dunes trail guides. If the kids did well on the hike, consider other similar, but more difficult, hikes in the dunes: Umpqua Dunes Trail, which crosses nearly 2 miles of open sand and passes dunes as high as 400 feet, and the Tahkenitch Dunes – Threemile Lake Loop, similar to the Overlook Loop but 6.5 miles long.

94. Sunset Bay–Cape Arago Shoreline

Type: Dayhike
Difficulty: Easy
Distance: 3.5 miles one way
Hikable: Year-round
Use: Heavy
High point: 50 feet
Elevation gain: 50 feet
Maps: USGS Cape Arago and
Charleston

Three contiguous state parks south of Charleston offer diverse opportunities to families, including swimming (or wading) in a protected cove, strolling through formal gardens, and picnicking on a bluff overlooking the Pacific. What most visitors to this area never see, however, is the dramatic, rocky shoreline that's only accessible by trail. So pull on some boots (it's muddy in places) and walk part or all of the Oregon Coast Trail between Sunset Bay Park, Shore Acres Park, and the viewpoint 0.5 mile north of Cape Arago. Hike as a one-way trek with a shuttle car, or make a round-trip hike from Sunset Bay to Shore Acres and back (3.6 miles).

From Charleston drive south, following signs, about 5 miles to Sunset
Bay Park. Park at the far end of the beach parking turnout, near the

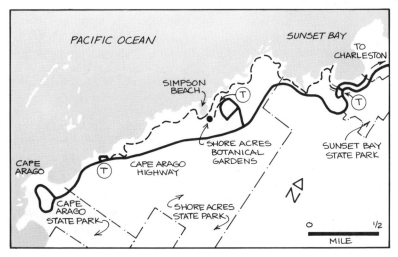

Shoreline between Sunset Bay and Shore Acres

restrooms, and look for a wooden post indicating the resumption of the Oregon Coast Trail. Cross the creek, then climb up onto the headland south of the bay. The trail reaches a big meadow on the left; follow the trail around it to the right, which leads along a bluff overlooking the ocean. Scramble trails lead down to a hidden beach here; they're rather treacherous-looking, but manageable with care.

At 0.6 mile the trail leads back out to the road (a spur trail leads down to a rocky cove frequented by surf anglers). Walk along the road 0.1 mile to a stile over the guardrail, where the trail resumes. A sign warns of the dangerous cliffs here, but the most treacherous drop-offs are discreetly fenced, and it's the road that's most dangerous. The trail follows a narrow strip between the cliffs and the road, then veers right to lead along the bluff, with grand views of Arago Lighthouse to the north and huge, wave-pounded rocks to the south. Scan the ocean for whales

or fishing boats, depending upon the season. At about 1.3 miles, the trail offers the first glimpse of the observation building at Shore Acres.

In another 0.5 mile the trail reaches some sandstone bluffs that compel exploration. Just above them is a cracked asphalt slab, evidence of the tennis courts built as part of the Shore Acres estate that's now a state park. Follow the path along the bluff, past the observation building. Either bear right, around the botanical gardens, or follow signs into the gardens for a side trip. (It may be possible to pick up the trail at the far end of the gardens if the gate there is open.)

The trail leads past Simpson Beach—a lovely, protected cove—and into the woods, then out onto the bluff. From October through May, listen, and later look, for the husky-voiced California sea lions that winter in large numbers here just offshore. At about 3.3 miles, the trail hits the road, follows it for about 50 yards, returns to the trail briefly, then ends a few steps north of a viewpoint 0.5 mile from the road's end at Cape Arago.

95. South Slough Estuary Loop

Type:	Dayhike
Difficulty:	Moderate
Distance:	2.5 to 5.3 miles, loop
Hikable:	Year-round
Use:	Light
High point:	320 feet
Elevation gain:	180 to 320 feet
Maps:	USGS Charleston; South Slough Estuary Study Trail

The South Slough of Coos Bay was designated a national estuarine reserve in 1974 to preserve this relatively complete estuarine system for study and recreation. The loop trail that leads down to the salt marsh and out onto old dikes in the estuary is peppered with interesting attractions along the way and loaded with simple teaching opportunities. It's a trail to linger on, with little side routes leading to even more points of interest. Begin with a stop at the visitor center, where displays geared for children help orient youngsters for what they'll see on the hike. Pick up a free trail guide here to enhance the hike. (If the visitor center is closed, trail guides may be found at the trailhead as well.)

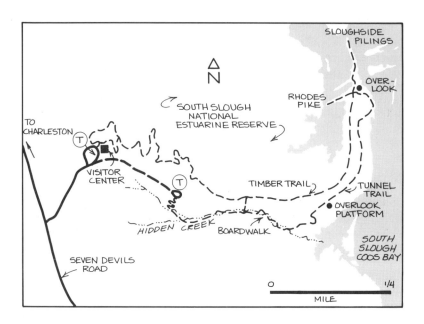

The trails at South Slough are continually being improved and extended; it's possible to find that the route has changed slightly from that outlined here, or that new trails have been constructed that permit exploration of different parts of the sanctuary. A couple of shorter trails, Winchester Creek and Wasson Creek, can help fill out a day of hiking at South Slough, and a marked canoe trail provides those traveling with a canoe another way to see the reserve.

In Charleston (about 8 miles southwest of Coos Bay) turn left at the sign to South Slough and drive 4.3 miles on Seven Devils Road to the entrance to the sanctuary, on the left. The visitor center is just ahead; the main trailhead is 0.2 mile down a signed spur road to the right. The hike also can be started at the visitor center, but about 1 mile is added on to the loop (and 140 feet elevation gain on the return).

From the main (lower) trailhead, follow the wood-chip path as it drops down to Hidden Creek. Cross the creek a few times before meeting the trail leading down from the visitor center at 0.4 mile (indicating the start of the loop). Bear right, continuing along the creek, which in March and April is bursting with bright-yellow (and faintly odorous) skunk cabbage. In a couple of minutes the trail meets a long boardwalk above the boggy creekbed, curving and winding among the skunk cabbage and through a corner of the salt marsh.

The trail resumes, leading to a large platform overlooking the marsh at 0.6 mile. It's hidden in the woods, serving as a kind of bird-watchers' blind; when they're through exploring the multilevel structure, encourage children not only to look for the movement of wings out in the marsh but to listen as well, for bird sounds or even human sounds, such as other hikers' voices or a faint "toot toot" indicating nearby logging operations.

Continuing, you'll find yourself on the Tunnel Trail section, bordered by dense understory vegetation closing in overhead much of the way. The trail passes restrooms at about 1 mile. Even the restrooms are a teaching

Boardwalk on South Slough nature trail

opportunity; they're furnished with Clivus Multram composting toilets, which turn the wastes they receive into usable compost in three years.

Continue hiking to another lookout point over the marsh, then down some steps to marsh level at about 1.2 miles. Here, encourage children to proceed as quietly as possible. Spur trails lead out along the marsh's edge and on top of a couple of old dikes; opportunities for spotting birds are excellent, if they aren't scared off first. The dikes were built years ago by homesteaders reclaiming the marsh for pastureland. Now they're slowly crumbling, as the estuary returns to its natural state.

To return, go straight on what's called the Timber Trail section rather than reclimb the stairs to the lookout over the marsh. The part-footpath, part-sand road gently winds back to a bench above Hidden Creek; follow signs back to either the lower trailhead or the visitor center.

96. Cape Sebastian

Type: Dayhike
Difficulty: Easy to moderate
Distance: 2.5 miles one way
Hikable: Year-round
Use: Heavy
High point: 700 feet
Elevation gain: 700 feet
Map: USGS Cape Sebastian

The hike out onto towering Cape Sebastian and down its south side to the beach is popular with locals as well as visitors. If possible, leave a car at Myers Creek wayside, 1.7 miles south of the turn-off to Cape Sebastian on U.S. 101, and hike the trail one way, mostly downhill. Otherwise, walk 0.4 mile out to the summit for awesome views of the south coast north and south, continuing down the cape as far down as everyone is willing to walk back up!

 From Gold Beach, take U.S. 101 south 5 miles and turn right at the sign to Cape Sebastian. Follow signs to the south viewpoint, where the trailhead takes off to the west.

The trail begins as an asphalt path dropping, then ascending, through a dense wall of wind-sculpted shrubbery; point out to children the kind of beating these plants take from the weather. Take a sniff: the ceanothus growing by the side of the trail is characteristic of the south coast and gives it a special perfume not found farther north. To the south, if the

Cape Sebastian

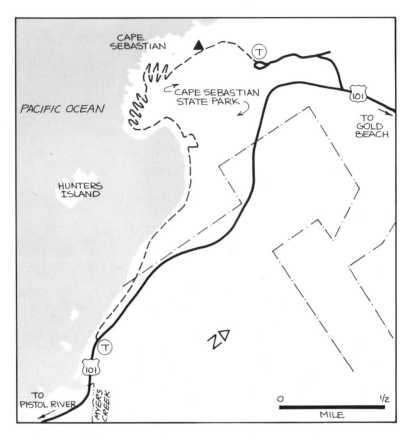

fog's absent, is a view of huge sea stacks and Hunters Island offshore. At 0.2 mile the pavement ends and the trail enters the trees, then emerges at the tip of the cape; look north to see the town of Gold Beach.

     The trail leads down the ridge to the south through a corridor of Sitka spruce, offering occasional views of the ocean as it switchbacks down through the gloomy forest. At about 1.5 miles, it emerges from the trees onto a bench above the bedrock, then continues to curve west, dropping onto the beach. Walk the beach south to where U.S. 101 meets the beach at Myers Creek wayside.

97. Boardman State Park: Indian Sands

Type:	Dayhike
Difficulty:	Easy
Distance:	0.4 mile to 5 miles round-trip
Hikable:	Year-round
Use:	Heavy
High point:	365 feet
Elevation gain:	580 feet
Map:	USGS Carpenterville

Boardman State Park is a great resource for hiking families with young children. The park is stretched out along the coastline between Pistol River and Brookings, with the Oregon Coast Trail running between the ocean and U.S. 101. Numerous trailheads are scattered along the highway, dividing the trail into sections ranging from about 0.5 mile to 3 miles. If willing to take a chance, just pull over at one of the signed viewpoints or trailhead parking areas and start walking; you really can't lose. Fall is a particularly nice time to hike here, as weather tends to be good and the trail not too brushy (it's rather overgrown in spring before trail crews arrive). Watch for poison oak, especially on the trail between Whaleshead Beach and Indian Sands.

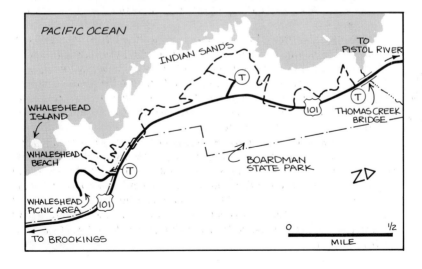

Shoreline off Boardman State Park

  One of the most interesting sections is known as Indian Sands, at about the middle of the park. For quick access to this area of sculptured sandstone cliffs, arches, and coves, pull into the Indian Sands parking area off U.S. 101 just south of milepost 348 (about 12 miles north of Brookings) and follow the trail 0.2 mile down through coastal forest to the shore. Emerging from the trees you'll find yourself in a fantasyland, where wind and water have sculpted the open dunes and ocher sandstone into marvelous shapes and land forms.

For a longer hike, include Indian Sands in a 2.5-mile hike from Thomas Creek Bridge south to Whaleshead Beach, or make a 1.7-mile hike from Indian Sands to Whaleshead Beach. A shuttle car provides the option of one-way hikes.

The northern trailhead, off the parking area at the south end of Thomas Creek Bridge, is south of milepost 347 off U.S. 101. The southern trailhead is at the top of the road leading off U.S. 101 to Whaleshead Beach, south of milepost 349.

  From Thomas Creek Bridge, follow the trail down a draw, through a forest of Sitka spruce, and across an open hillside. The trail swings back to U.S. 101 at 0.5 mile. Walk along the highway a short distance, then pick up the trail again, following it down a steep draw. It's more dramatic than hazardous in here, but keep an eye on children. Turn a corner, climb over a saddle, and follow posts through the sand a short distance to Indian Sands, at about 1 mile.

Continue south, following the posts, to where the trail resumes, leading into shady woods. It crosses a couple of creeks, then leads out to the highway 0.8 mile from Indian Sands. Walk south inside the guardrail about 40 yards until the trail resumes in a salal-bordered corridor leading into a forest of Sitka spruce. The trail climbs a bit, then offers a peek into a hidden cove. Round a corner to get a grand view of Whaleshead Beach, then switchback down to the parking area at the top of the road to Whaleshead.

To extend the outing, follow the paved road a short distance down to the beach. Walk south on the beach 1 mile to pick up the Oregon Coast Trail again.

98. Redwood Nature Trail

Type: Dayhike
Difficulty: Easy to moderate
Distance: 1.5 to 3 miles, loop
Hikable: Year-round
Use: Light
High point: 470 feet
Elevation gain: 370 feet
Map: USGS Mt. Emily

There's something special about being in a redwood forest—children sense it as quickly as adults. The big trees with their reddish bark and lacy-needle boughs draping loftily overhead create a magical atmosphere.

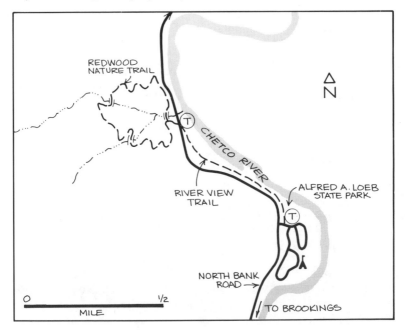

Redwood Nature Trail

This trail is all the more fun because it's unexpected. First, redwoods are supposed to be in California, not Oregon. (These are actually the northernmost redwoods in the world.) Second, the lushness of the forest here, a few miles inland, contrasts sharply with the open headlands of the south coast for those traveling along U.S. 101. The hike is short, but there are some fairly steep stretches, making it feel more like a real hike than just a nature walk.

From the south end of Brookings, turn east from U.S. 101 onto North Bank Road and drive 7.8 miles to Alfred A. Loeb State Park. Start hiking here, following the 0.75-mile River View Trail that leads along a narrow corridor between the Chetco River and road to end across the road from the start of the Redwood Nature Trail. Or drive 0.6 mile farther to the trailhead, on the left (where there is room for about two cars).

Pick up an interpretive pamphlet, if available, at the station by the toilet just up the trail. Shortly the trail reaches a junction; turn left to hike clockwise, following the order of numbered posts, which correspond with explanations in the trail pamphlet. The brochure focuses mostly on natural history but weaves in some human history as well; one post marks an old log-cage bear trap built years ago and long abandoned.

For the first 0.5 mile, Douglas firs predominate along the trail as it ascends steadily. After crossing a footbridge over the creek, you'll start seeing big redwoods and lots of rhododendrons. The trail peaks at about 0.75 mile. Cross the creek again, then start switchbacking down through the forest to recross the creek and meet the start of the loop.

Index

THE MOUNTAINEERS, founded in 1906, is a non-profit outdoor activity and conservation club, whose mission is "to explore, study, preserve and enjoy the natural beauty of the outdoors...." Based in Seattle, Washington, the club is now the third largest such organization in the United States, with 15,000 members and five branches throughout Washington State.

The Mountaineers sponsors both classes and year-round outdoor activities in the Pacific Northwest, which include hiking, mountain climbing, ski-touring, snowshoeing, bicycling, camping, kayaking and canoeing, nature study, sailing, and adventure travel. The club's conservation division supports environmental causes through educational activities, sponsoring legislation, and presenting informational programs. All club activities are led by skilled, experienced volunteers, who are dedicated to promoting safe and responsible enjoyment and preservation of the outdoors.

The Mountaineers Books, an active, non-profit publishing program of the club, produces guidebooks, instructional texts, historical works, natural history guides, and works on environmental conservation. All books produced by The Mountaineers are aimed at fulfilling the club's mission.

If you would like to participate in these organized outdoor activities or the club's programs, consider a membership in The Mountaineers. For information and an application, write or call The Mountaineers, Club Headquarters, 300 Third Avenue West, Seattle, Washington 98119; (206) 284-6310.

BONNIE HENDERSON grew up in Portland, Oregon, and spent most family vacations hiking and backpacking in Mount Hood National Forest. During college she began guiding whitewater raft trips and leading teenagers on wilderness backpacking trips in the Rocky, Cascade, and Olympic mountains, and later taught cross-country skiing at Mount St. Helens. Three years as a newspaper reporter led her to pursue a master's degree in journalism, followed by six years as a travel writer with *Sunset* magazine, focusing on outdoor recreation in the Northwest. She is now a writer and editor living in Eugene.